I. PRIMARY REFERENCE WORKS ON SHAKESPEARE

II. CRITICISM AND INTERPRETATION

    A. Textual Treatises, Commentaries
    B. Treatment of Specal Subjects
    C. Dramatic and Literary Art in Shakespeare

III. SHAKESPEARE AND HIS TIME

    A. General Treatises. Biography
    B. The Age of Shakespeare
    C. Authorship

Series II, Part A

HAMLET
AND THE SCOTTISH SUCCESSION

𝕷ibrary of 𝕾hakespearean 𝕭iography and 𝕮riticism

HAMLET

AND

THE SCOTTISH SUCCESSION

BEING AN EXAMINATION OF THE RELATIONS OF
THE PLAY OF *HAMLET* TO THE SCOTTISH
SUCCESSION AND THE ESSEX CONSPIRACY

BY

LILIAN WINSTANLEY

 BOOKS FOR LIBRARIES PRESS
FREEPORT, NEW YORK

First Published 1921
Reprinted 1970

STANDARD BOOK NUMBER:
8369-5270-7

LIBRARY OF CONGRESS CATALOG CARD NUMBER:
78-109661

PRINTED IN THE UNITED STATES OF AMERICA

In Memoriam

THOMAS FRANCIS ROBERTS,

D.LITT., LL.D.

Principal of the University College of Wales

Aberystwyth

1891–1919

" Revered as a teacher, beloved as a friend, and
remembered as an inspiration."

" Ei fywyd yn fflam dros Addysg ei wlad."

PREFACE

I wish to thank my historical colleagues at Aberystwyth for the sympathy and help they have given me during the writing of the following essay: Mr Sidney Herbert for recommending books, Dr E. A. Lewis for his invaluable assistance in directing me to *State Papers* and many other contemporary documents, and especially to Professor Stanley Roberts for reading my proofs, for giving me much information on Elizabethan history, and for his unfailing kindness in discussion and criticism.

Lilian Winstanley

The University College of Wales,
Aberystwyth, *November* 1920

CONTENTS

HAMLET AND THE
SCOTTISH SUCCESSION

(BEING AN EXAMINATION OF THE RELATIONS OF THE PLAY
OF *HAMLET* TO THE SCOTTISH SUCCESSION AND THE
ESSEX CONSPIRACY)

INTRODUCTION

IT is the purpose of the following essay to study the
play of *Hamlet* from a somewhat fresh point of view by
endeavouring to show its relation or possible relation to
contemporary history.

My attempt throughout has been to regard the play as
it naturally would be regarded by an Elizabethan audience,
for it seems to me that this particular angle of vision has
hitherto been too little considered in our current criticism.
We have not sufficiently realised, I think, that to consider
the Elizabethan audience is our least indirect method of
approach to Shakespeare himself. A dramatic poet
cannot possibly ignore the mentality of his audience;
an epic poet may, if he pleases, write, as we know Milton
actually did write, for posterity and for an audience " fit
though few "; but a dramatic poet who does genuinely
produce his plays before a popular audience cannot
possibly do anything of the kind. The mentality of his
audience provides him with at least half of his material.
It is through that mentality that his plays must be

reviewed and considered; it is to that mentality they must all appeal. If the dramatic poet wishes to discuss problems his task is immensely facilitated by selecting problems in which his audience are already interested; if he wishes to awaken feelings of terror and pathos, as every true dramatist must, his task is immensely facilitated if he appeals to associations already existing in their minds.

The mentality of his audience everywhere shapes and conditions his work as certainly as the work of a sculptor is shaped by the architecture and purpose of the building in which it stands. The sculpture of the Parthenon is not more certainly adapted to the purpose of the Parthenon than are the plays of a true dramatist to the mentality of his audience.

Now, in the case of Shakespeare, the mentality of the audience is doubly important, because there is no direct method of approach. Shakespeare himself has left no letters or prefaces which explain his work; his contemporaries have left no criticisms; the notices we possess of his plays are extremely meagre and most of them limited, like those of Forman, to a mere reference to the subject of the play.

Neither can we judge Shakespeare completely by the effect produced on our own minds; we, after all, are a remote posterity, and nothing is more certain than that he did not write for us. We ourselves may be quite adequate judges of the purely æsthetic effect of the plays; but, in order to understand them fully, it is surely necessary to ask what their effect upon a contemporary audience would be likely to be and what such an audience would probably think they meant.

The moment we attempt to place ourselves at the same angle of vision as an Elizabethan audience we see many things in a different light ; many problems solve themselves quite simply ; but, on the other hand, many are suggested which do not occur to the modern reader, and which nevertheless surely demand solution if we are to comprehend Shakespeare fully and completely.

I propose to give illustrations of both types of problems, of those which solve themselves and of those which suggest themselves.

Let us enquire, for instance, why Shakespeare selected the subject of Macbeth ? One reason is obvious. A Scottish king had recently succeeded to the throne and the choice of a Scottish theme was, in itself, a compliment to him. Then, again, Banquo was the ancestor of the Stuarts, and the subject of the play enables Shakespeare to depict Banquo in a favourable light.

But is there any reason for the selection of Macbeth himself as a hero ?

There is, I think, an exceedingly good one ; but it only becomes evident after a careful study of the ideas of the epoch.

Macbeth was the person who fulfilled the Merlin prophecies and, by so doing, brought about the foundation of the British Empire. The Merlin prophecies, as interpreted by the so-called Tudor bards, were to the effect that the ancient British line should once again succeed to the throne of England and that, when it did so succeed, the different British kingdoms should be united under one crown and the ancient Arthurian empire restored. Professor Gwynn Jones assures me that these Merlin prophecies had an important political bearing in sixteenth-century Wales ; they certainly had in England, and they were celebrated by many poets, notably Spenser, Drayton, and Ben Jonson.

Drayton's lines happen to be the most apposite for my purpose, so I quote them :

> " the ancient British race
> Shall come again to sit upon the sovereign place. . . .
> By Tudor, with fair winds from little Britaine driven,
> To whom the goodly bay of Milford shall be given ;
> As thy wise prophets, Wales, foretold his wish'd arrive
> And how Lewellin's line in him should doubly thrive.
> For from his issue sent to Albany before,
> Where his neglected blood his virtue did restore
> He first unto himself in fair succession gained
> The Stewards nobler name ; and afterwards attained
> The royal Scottish wreath, upholding it in state.
> This stem, to Tudors joined . . .
> Suppressing every Plant, shall spread itself so wide
> As in his arms shall clip the Isle on every side,
> By whom three severed realms in one shall firmly stand
> As Britain-founding Brute first monarchised the Land." [1]

Selden's note on the above passage is : " About our Confessor's time, Macbeth, King of Scotland (moved by prediction, affirming that his line extinct, the posterity of Banquho, a noble thane of Loqhuabre, should attain and continue the Scottish reign) and, jealous of others, hoped—for greatness, murdered Banquho, but missed his design ; for one of the same posterity, Fleanch son to Banquho, privily fled to Gryffith ap Llewelin (Drayton *Polyolbion*, Song V.), then Prince of Wales, and was there kindly received.   To him and Nesta, the Prince's daughter,

---

[1] Drayton, *Polyolbion*, Song V.

was issue one Walter. . . . The rest alludes to that :
Cambria shall be glad, Cornwall shall flourish, and the
Isle shall be styled with Brute's name and the name of
strangers shall perish : as it is in Merlin's prophecies."

We are now in a position to see what Macbeth really
meant to the Elizabethans : he was the man who fulfilled the Merlin prophecies, and he fulfilled them by the
very fact that he tried to evade them ; when Fleance,
the son of the murdered Banquho, fled to Wales he inter-
married with the ancient British line and thus brought
its blood to the throne of Scotland.

Now the Elizabethans always laid immense stress on
this genealogy for their monarchs ; anyone who will
refer to Camden's genealogy of the Tudors will see that
he derives their line from Brutus the Trojan, and the
Stuarts, as we have just seen from Drayton and Selden,
were similarly derived through Fleance the son of
Banquho.

Now an Elizabethan audience would surely see in
Macbeth the same theme as in the lines quoted from
Drayton. We have the enormous stress laid on prophecy
throughout the play, we have the question of the succession
prominent in Macbeth's mind, we have the murder of
Banquho and the flight of Fleance, we have the future
shown to Macbeth with the progeny of this Fleance
succeeding, and we have the vision of the unity of the
British Isles in the procession of the kings who " two-
fold balls and treble-sceptres carry " and whose lines
" stretch out to the crack of doom."

Macbeth has, then, the same theme as the passage
already quoted from Drayton ; what they both deal

with is the founding or, as they would have put it, the restoration of the British Empire.

The main conception is exactly similar to those which occur in Greek tragedy, where the very attempt to evade prophecy brings about its fulfilment, and the theme is as intimately interwoven with British history in the widest and truest sense of the term as any theme selected by a Greek dramatist was interwoven with Greek history. It is difficult to imagine any subject more appropriate to render before James I. ; he was the destined restorer of the ancient Arthurian empire, the man destined to unite England, Scotland, Wales and Ireland all under the same crown, as long ago prophesied by Merlin, and the play shows how the effort to avert the succession from the line of Banquho led precisely to its fulfilment.[1]

Or let me choose another illustration. Suppose we ask whether Shakespeare's Denmark, as depicted in *Hamlet*, is a real country or not and, if real, what country! Everyone will admit that Denmark makes a singularly real and vivid impression upon the mind ; it is as real, in the dramatic sense, as any country we have ever known or heard of. But did Shakespeare invent it as a background for his melancholy prince, or was he describing any country he knew? It certainly is not the Denmark of his source ; the Denmark of Saxo Grammaticus is an almost entirely barbaric country, savage and primitive to a degree ; even the Hamlet, the hero of the primitive story, cuts an enemy's body to pieces and boils it and outrages a woman, and yet he is the best person in

[1] See note *A*, Appendix.

the whole piece. Is Shakespeare's Denmark, then, an
imaginary region created by himself ?

Let us ask what an Elizabethan audience would have
made of it. I do not think there need be five minutes'
delay about the answer to this question. An Elizabethan
audience would almost certainly have thought Denmark
a real country, and they would have believed it to be
contemporary Scotland.

The peculiar combination of circumstances and the
peculiar type of manners depicted in Shakespeare's
Denmark are, in the highest degree, distinctive and
strange; but they can every one be paralleled in the case
of sixteenth-century Scotland.

Shakespeare's Denmark, to begin with, is a country
where feudal anarchy reigns ; there is no settled law and
order : the crown is seized by a usurper and almost every
principal personage—the elder Hamlet, the younger
Hamlet, Polonius, Claudius, the Queen—ends either by
a violent death or by assassination.

So also was Scotland a feudal anarchy. So also were
the powers of the crown in Scotland in continual danger
of being seized by usurpers and insurgents as in the case
of the elder Bothwell and the younger Bothwell: in
Scotland also almost every monarch or prominent states-
man did meet either with a tragic and premature death,
or with a death by assassination. James V., Mary Queen
of Scots, Darnley, Rizzio, Murray—these were only the
most prominent among a number of tragedies : assassination was, indeed, the recognised method by which a great
noble removed a rival.

Shakespeare has been blamed for the " holocaust of

dead " in *Hamlet*; but it is not one whit more remark-able than the mass of assassinations in sixteenth-century Scottish history.   The English of Shakespeare's day had a bitter prejudice against Scotland, and very largely on account of this anarchy.

Yet Shakespeare's Denmark is no mere barbaric country ; it is distinguished by its love of education, its philo-sophical depth, and its power of thought and meditation. Of all Shakespeare's tragedies *Hamlet* is admittedly the most philosophic and the most profound ; this has no parallel whatever in the original saga, but it has a parallel in contemporary Scotland.

Knox and his body of reformers had already commenced that educational revival which was to make Scotland one of the most admirably educated countries in Europe ; their intellectual interests were largely of a philosophical character.

Now, it is the *combination* of these circumstances which is so peculiar, which is indeed unique, and it is precisely this peculiar *combination* which appears in Shakespeare's *Hamlet*.

Moreover, it should be noted that Shakespeare's Denmark is quite manifestly a country where the Catholic faith and the Protestant exist side by side ; the ghost is certainly a Catholic, for he laments nothing more than the fact that he was not allowed absolution at his death, that he was

> " Cut off even in the blossoms of my sin,
> Unhousel'd, disappointed, unaneled,
> No reckoning made but sent to my account
> With all my imperfections on my head."

On the other hand, Hamlet is just as plainly a Protestant : he has been a fellow-student with Horatio at Wittenberg, and it is to Wittenberg he wishes to return. Now Wittenberg, on account of its connection with Luther, was one of the most famous of Protestant Universities.

This peculiar combination is, once again, exactly paralleled in contemporary Scotland; the queen's party were Catholics; her opponents were the Protestant lords, and there was a specially close connection between Scotland and German Protestant Universities. Knox himself once had a congregation at Frankfort-on-the-Main,[1] and there were many other Scotch Protestants in different parts of Germany. " There was a whole Scoto-German school, among whom the Wedderburns were predominant."

Again, Shakespeare's Denmark is a place where the king has been murdered and his wife has married the murderer. This also happened in sixteenth-century Scotland; Darnley is almost invariably alluded to in contemporary documents (Buchanan's *Oration and Detection*, for instance), as the " king "; the " king " had been murdered, and his wife had married the murderer.

Shakespeare's Denmark also is a place where a councillor is murdered in the presence of a queen, and his body disposed of " hugger-mugger " fashion by a staircase. This, also, had happened in contemporary Scotland in the case of Rizzio's murder.

I shall show later that in both these cases the resemblances between the history and Shakespeare are much more close than any possible resemblances with the saga source.

Moreover, Shakespeare's Denmark is a place where there is, apparently, no army at the king's disposal, and

[1] Froude, Chap. X.

where, when discontented nobles desire the redress of grievances, they enter the palace at the head of an armed band, and threaten the king's person, as happens with Laertes and Claudius. This was positively the recognised method of conducting an opposition in sixteenth-century Scotland. When a powerful subject had a grievance, he did at once put himself at the head of an armed band, and either threaten the person of the king or attempt to seize upon the person of the king.

Then, again, there is the love of strong drink which is so marked a feature in Shakespeare's Denmark, and the drunken carousals. This also was characteristic of a certain conspicuous group in sixteenth-century Scotland ; Buchanan continually calls the elder Bothwell a drunken beast.[1]

Moreover, the resemblance extends even to the smallest details. Shakespeare's Denmark shows both Italian and Danish names at court ; so did contemporary Scotland, there was a Guildenstern (like Shakespeare's), and a Francesco (like Shakespeare's), the latter being a friend of Rizzio's.

Now it seems to me that, with all these resemblances quite obvious and on the surface, an Elizabethan audience would almost certainly assume either that Shakespeare was deliberately depicting contemporary Scotland, or, at the very least, that he was deliberately borrowing many of its distinctive traits. The resemblances range from the most inclusive circumstances to the smallest details— they embrace the peculiar combinations of feudal anarchy and philosophy, of strong drink and of students at German

[1] *Oration and Detection.*

universities, and they even include a Danish Guildenstern and an Italian Francesco.

And, further, is there anything strange in such a resemblance? Why should *not* Shakespeare wish to depict sixteenth-century Scotland? It was a country in which Shakespeare's audience were intensely interested: it was the country which was just about to provide them with a king; it was a country whose crown was to be intimately associated with theirs; a study of its leading traits would be likely to interest Shakespeare's audience more than any other subject which, at that particular date, it would be possible for him to choose.

Another example may be chosen from *The Merchant of Venice*. It is very generally admitted that Shakespeare's portrait of a Jew villain is probably in part due to the great excitement caused by the trial of a Jew, Roderigo Lopez, for the attempted murder of the queen and Don Antonio: Lopez was executed in 1594.

Shakespeare, in drawing the portrait of the Jew villain, was availing himself of what was just then a strong popular excitement against the Jews. So much is admitted! [1]

But surely the play suggests a good deal more. Antonio was a claimant to the throne of Portugal and, as the rival claimant was Philip II., Antonio became, on this account, a very popular person with the majority of the Elizabethans, who hated Philip and instinctively took the side of anyone opposed to him. Antonio had come to London, bringing with him exceedingly valuable jewels; his purpose was to pledge these with the merchants

[1] See Boas, *Shakespeare and His Predecessors*.

of London, and so to procure the money for ships to fight Philip of Spain. The Essex and Southampton party—Shakespeare's patrons—were keenly in favour of a forward policy against Spain and consequently in favour of Antonio. On the other hand, Elizabeth and Burleigh desired peace ; Antonio was allowed to pledge his jewels but, on one pretext or another, he was prevented from getting his ships. He was thus in the position of a ruined bankrupt, and popular feeling ran high in his favour.

Essex started, on his own account, a system of espionage which was deliberately intended to rival that of Burleigh. His spies discovered evidence that there was a Spanish plot to poison the queen and Don Antonio by using the physician—Lopez, as an intermediary. Elizabeth, at first, refused wholly to credit the existence of such a plot and blamed Essex as a " rash and temerarious youth," for bringing accusations against the innocent. Essex, however, persisted ; fresh evidence was procured, a public trial was ordered, and Lopez was condemned to death. Still the queen delayed, and it was three months before she could be induced to sign the death-warrant. Even then she exercised her prerogative so far as to allow the family of Lopez to retain a considerable portion of his wealth.

Lopez had professed himself a Christian.

As Naunton points out Elizabeth was regarded as a most merciful princess. We may remember that one of Spenser's names for her was " Mercilla." [1] Now this tendency to mercy seemed to the public to have been exercised too far in the Lopez affair.

[1] *Faerie Queene*, Bk. V

We might also observe that Don Antonio himself was partly Jewish ; he was the son of a Jewess who had become converted to Christianity.

Now, surely, we have here very remarkable parallels to Shakespeare's play ?

We have Don Antonio who has been a very wealthy man but who has practically become a bankrupt through losses incurred over his own ships ; a Jew forms a plot against his life and nearly succeeds, but it is discovered, and the Jew punished.

So Shakespeare's hero is an Antonio ; he also has been wealthy, but is reduced, apparently, to bankruptcy by losses over his ships. So does a Jew attempt his life ; so is the plot frustrated.

We have Elizabeth, who will not believe in the guilt of the Jew, who makes every attempt to show him mercy, who delays almost intolerably over his trial, but who is compelled to give sentence in the end ; we have the fact that she was famous for mercy, and that one of her poetic names was " Mercilla."

So Shakespeare gives us Portia, who will not believe in the guilt of the Jew, who gives him every possible opportunity, who identifies herself with mercy in the noblest of all poetic praises ; but who is compelled, finally, to give sentence.

We have in the play, just as in the history, the fact that the fine upon the Jew's goods is remitted, and that they are allowed to pass to his children. Moreover, in the life of Don Antonio, in the fact that his mother was a Jewess who married a Christian, we have a parallel to another most interesting episode in Shakespeare's play ; that of Lorenzo and Jessica.

Is it not probable that Shakespeare selected his material and chose his plot largely that his play might appeal to interests then paramount in the minds of his audience ?

Surely nothing can be more plausible ?

We have even, in Bassanio, a parallel to the situation of Essex himself ; he is the friend of Antonio ; he is the soldier, the man of noble birth but without fortune, who quite frankly approaches Portia to " repair his fortunes." So was Essex the friend of Don Antonio ; so had Essex hoped to profit by his ships, so was Essex a soldier, young and of noble birth, but poor ; so did he approach Elizabeth in the frank hope of mending his fortunes.

We also observe that, if Shakespeare be really drawing parallels with history, many of the adverse criticisms on his play find at least their explanation.

Thus there is simply no point in sentimentalising over his cruelty in compelling Shylock to become a Christian ; the actual historic Jew had professed Christianity and did profess it to the end. Neither need we blame him for allowing Portia to drag out the trial scene so intolerably and " get on the nerves " of the spectators ; it was just precisely this delay which had " got on the nerves " of the Elizabethan public. Neither need we wonder that Shakespeare allows Portia to give judgment in the Duke's own court : it *was* with Elizabeth that the matter finally rested.

Is it not easy to see that Shakespeare has taken his literary source and has dovetailed into it a great deal of history as well ? [1]

Another incident I will select is from *Henry IV.*, Part II —the famous incident of the repudiation of Falstaff.

[1] See note *B*, Appendix.

In scene after scene throughout the plays we have seen Henry rejoicing himself with the inimitable wit of Falstaff, treating him as his boon companion, and as one of his most intimate friends ; then, on his accession, he repudiates him publicly and orders him to be haled off to prison, for we hear the Chief Justice giving the order : " Go, carry Sir John Falstaff to the Fleet." Is not this needlessly harsh and stern ? How often has this particular point been debated ! Some of Shakespeare's critics do accuse Henry of unnecessary harshness ; a number of others find a way out by protesting that it was essential for Henry to effect a complete severance from Falstaff. Do they think Shakespeare's hero-king such a moral weakling that he could not guard himself against the temptations of " sack and sugar " except by putting the tempter in prison ?

The truth is that the passage, as it stands, is a perpetual puzzle to the modern reader who finds Falstaff a very fascinating personage, sympathises with him, and is convinced that Henry, whatever grounds he may have had for repudiating Falstaff, cannot have had any for imprisoning him.

The explanation, I take it, is again historic. The kings of the house of Lancaster had an exceedingly bad title in point of law ; they won the all-powerful support of the Church only by engaging in a perpetual heresy-hunt ; hence the many Lollard trials of the reign of Henry V. Now we know that in the original version of the play, Falstaff was called Oldcastle, and Sir John Oldcastle was the greatest of all Lollard leaders.

The fact of his imprisonment was simply a historic

fact, and the audience knew well enough the reasons for it ; the historic Henry had strained himself to the utmost in the effort to save his old friend from the ire of enraged ecclesiastics, and, even when he was imprisoned, had tried to persuade him to recant. How could the audience think Henry severe when they knew that the true offence was a political one, and that a continuance of the friendship on Henry's part would have brought down the dynasty ? Surely this sheds a different light on Henry ?

It also throws light on other portions of the play. Falstaff repeatedly claims a great reputation for military skill, a European reputation in fact, for he says that he is " Sir John to all Europe." Now a good many critics treat this as simple absurdity on his part, but it is perfectly accurate ; *Oldcastle* was *acknowledged* as one of the greatest soldiers of his day. Whether Shakespeare meant him to *deserve* his reputation or not is an entirely different point, but he certainly possessed it. Canon Ainger has shown that a great deal in the character of Falstaff can be explained by the fact that the Elizabethan conception of him was that of a renegade Puritan, and it is surely equally appropriate to remember that he had the reputation of being a great soldier. That is the joke of the battle of Shrewsbury.[1] That is precisely why he is able to claim, with any hope of credence, that he killed Hotspur, and that is preceisely why Sir John Colevile of the Dale surrenders to his reputation only.[2]

In all these cases the historic method helps us, I think, very markedly to understand the plays in question ;

[1] *Henry IV.*, Part I.   [2] *Henry IV.*, Part II.

on the other hand, we are bound to admit that, if we study the peculiar point of view of the Elizabethan mind, problems are often suggested where all might otherwise to the modern reader appear plain. It seems to me, however, that it is at least equally necessary to study the problems which thus arise. How can we be sure that we understand him fully if we ignore the manner in which his plays and his subjects were likely to affect contemporary minds? I will give two instances where important problems suggest themselves which have not, I think, as yet been resolved.

Let us consider, for instance, the identity of Lear. Lear appears in Geoffrey of Monmouth as the king who founded the city of Leicester, and it is ultimately, though not directly, from Geoffrey of Monmouth that Shakespeare's version of the story is derived. Shakespeare has, however, altered the conclusion and linked the whole with an entirely different tale—the history of Gloucester and his sons—whose source is Sidney's *Arcadia.* Now Lear is not only a character in Geoffrey of Monmouth; he is also an important figure in Welsh mythology where his daughter—Cordelia—has as rival wooers Modred and Gwynn ap Nudd, the prince of fairyland; these two are doomed to fight for her every first of May until the Day of Judgment.

In Irish mythology also Lear or Lir plays an important part, and his children are turned into wild swans.

Now what is Lear's real identity?

Sir John Rhys states that Lir is a Celtic sea-god; Mr Timothy Lewis tells me that he thinks this a mistake, that Lir is a noun used as an adjective and means the

B

Ligurian Sea only, but not any other : Lear or Lir really means the Ligures tribes ; there were a number of such personages in ancient Welsh ; they are called the fathers of the British race, and they really mean the invading tribes from the Continent.

Now it may not be of importance to our Shakespearian study to know what Lear really and essentially is ; but it is surely of considerable importance to know what the Elizabethans thought he was.

Was Lear a man or a god or a tribe ? This question is not even asked. The majority of critics are like Mr Bradley, they start with the assumption that Lear was an ancient British king, and they do not even discuss the possibility that the Elizabethans understood Lear as a mythologic figure and that Shakespeare himself may have meant him as something mythologic.

Mr Bradley's omission to ask the question is the more curious because he himself admits that Lear produces on his mind the impression of being strangely remote from ordinary life ; the tale, as such, is extravagantly improbable and yet the drama is enormously great.

" This world," says Mr Bradley, " is called Britain ; but we should no more look for it than for the place called Caucasus, where Prometheus was chained by Strength and Force and comforted by the daughters of Ocean."

And elsewhere he says that he finds that he is often grouping the play in his own mind " with works like the *Prometheus Vinctus*, and the *Divine Comedy* and even with the greatest symphonies of Beethoven and the statues in the Medici Chapel."

In other words, the play makes an impression closely resembling that of mythologic symbolism. Very well! is it not possible that Shakespeare's audience would have conceived Lear as a figure in mythology?

Or consider Othello as another case where the Elizabethan point of view very naturally suggests a problem. From Coleridge to Mr Bradley most of our critics assume that Othello is meant to be a noble character.

Mr Bradley says: "This character is so noble, Othello's actions and feeling follow so inevitably from it—and his sufferings are so heartrending that he stirs I believe, in most readers, a passion of mingled love and pity which they feel for no other hero in Shakespeare."

Now, it is impossible to deny that this " noble " person commits great crimes; he murders an innocent and devoted wife, and plans the murder of a loyal friend; it is quite true that Cassio's assassination is averted, but that is sheer accident; it is not owing to any repentance in Othello, and Othello remains morally guilty of two murders, both of innocent people.

These are undeniably great crimes; still the whole tendency of our modern criticism is to lay all the stress upon Iago's villainy and to regard Othello as being almost wholly a victim. But now let us make one enquiry! Such a subject is, in itself, an excellent dramatic subject, and it is easy enough to understand Shakespeare's choice. But why if it be really his intention to show us an innocent noble husband driven to the murder of an innocent wife, why does he commence with making his hero a Moor? The audience of the sixteenth century had an intense prejudice against Moors, a prejudice at least as strong as an audience of to-day would have against Prussian officers.

The Moors were, in the sixteenth century, the most formidable opponents of Christian Europe ; their valour had threatened its complete overthrow, and since they were heathen and formidable opponents at one and the same time, they were regarded as the accepted types of villainy. We see this in the second book of Spenser's *Faerie Queene*, where the three Saracens are the most formidable opponents of the knight Guyon ; we see it in Shakespeare's own *Titus Andronicus* where the Moor is represented as absolutely black, and also a villain of the most dreadful type.

Even modern critics like Coleridge and Charles Lamb feel a distinct repulsion. Coleridge argues that Othello cannot have been really black, but must have been brown ; I need not repeat his arguments, for every one knows them, and they are all contradicted by the simple fact that Shakespeare makes the Moor Aaron absolutely black.

Then, again, Charles Lamb says that he prefers Othello for reading rather than for representation on the stage, because on the stage his black face alienates the sympathy of the audience. Of course it does. But the prejudice excited in Charles Lamb's mind must have been as nothing compared to the prejudices excited in the minds of an Elizabethan audience for whom a Moor's black face was simply the accepted symbol for the villainy of a Moor's black soul.

Try and imagine a dramatic author of to-day doing anything really comparable ! Try and imagine him representing a hero who murders an innocent wife and attempts the murder of an innocent friend ; supposing that, notwithstanding these dreadful facts, he wishes to awaken the utmost sympathy for the murderous hero. Will be begin by making his hero a Prussian officer ? Of course not ! Our dramatist knows perfectly well that his audience have a prejudice against Prussian officers of the intensest possible kind, that they will certainly, from the very outset, consider the hero a villain and that they will certainly, from the very outset, expect him to do something unjust and abominable. Surely no dramatist would so far stultify his own dramatic intention ?

And yet even the case of the Prussian officer is not strong enough, for it does not include the colour bar. Imagine a Prussian officer who is also a negro, and imagine the play acted before an audience of Southern State Americans ! And that the parallel is really true and really just anyone can see by simply referring to Shakespeare's source. In Cinthio's novel the conclusion drawn is exactly the one that might have been expected ; the noble Venetian lady marries the Moor, notwithstanding the prohibition of her parents, and the result is what might have been anticipated—a cruel murder.

Now, how do our critics get out of this difficulty ? They never meet it fairly. They simply assume, like Mr Bradley, that Shakespeare was gloriously original, gloriously in advance of his age. This, when we consider the character of the villainous Moor Aaron seems very doubtful ; but, even supposing Shakespeare were free from the prejudices of his age, was his *audience* free ? That is the real crux of the whole matter. Mr Bradley admits that even Coleridge could not rise to the " full glory " of Shakespeare's conception. How, then, does Mr Bradley think the Elizabethan audience could rise to it ? Were they less free from race prejudice than Coleridge, the devotee of the rights of man ?

Moreover, the whole difficulty was so needless ! Assuming that all Shakespeare wished to do was to write a story of love and murderous jealousy, he could have easily found scores and scores of such tales which were intrinsically better material than Cinthio's novel. The one thing that is peculiar about Cinthio's novel is the fact that the hero is a Moor ; in other words, Shakespeare chose precisely the story which included the one thing likely to wreck his dramatic effect at the outset. Is this probable ?

Is it not possible that Othello is really meant to be a villain, and that his great qualities are like the great qualities of Macbeth—things which do not prevent the rest of the man from being evil ?

At any rate the difficulty should be fairly answered, and I submit that we cannot do this without a most careful historic study.

Moreover, as soon as we take the Elizabethan point of view, another question at once suggests itself. Are we justified in interpreting Shakespeare, as completely as we do, from a modern psychological standpoint ?

It is quite true that every era which is interested in human nature must have its own method of psychology ; but this psychology also has its historical development and the method of one age differs considerably from the method of another.

Let anyone who doubts this take the simplest of tests. Let him turn to Pope, who explains his own psychology in the *Moral Essays, The Essay on Man,* and elsewhere. The virtue of human life depends on a right balance between passion and reason and, according to him, the key to character is to be found in the " ruling passion "— to discover a man's ruling passion is to know him. Now, Pope's own method of character-drawing depends on his own psychology, and is to be explained by that psychology ; but it is quite obsolete for us. Who now thinks of the " ruling passion " as the key to a man's character ?

But if the method of the Queen Anne period is so far obsolete, should we not expect the method of the Elizabethans to be more obsolete still ?

Let us take an Elizabethan example in Ben Jonson's *Comedy of Humours.*

This is how Mr Gregory Smith explains Jonson's psychology : [1] " In the older physiology the four major humours, corresponding with the four elements—formed according to their proportionate allowances in each body— the " temperament " or " complexion " or " constitution " of a man, and declared his character. Variations in the relative strength of these humours disclosed the individual differences. These differences might be great or small in respect of one or more of the contributing humours. By simple arithmetic it was easy to show that great odds were against any two men having the same formula of temperament ; and so the theory fitted itself comfortably to experience."

[1] *Ben Jonson.*

Now, this was the psychology of one of Shakespeare's own contemporaries. If Ben Jonson's psychology was, to our own thinking, as extraordinary as this, what was Shakespeare's psychology ? Surely we ought to explain *his* method ? Pope's interpretation of character depends upon the theory of the ruling passion, which he regards as the key to it. Ben Jonson's interpretation of character depends upon " humours." Both these methods are obsolete for us. Are our critics likely to be right when they represent Shakespeare almost entirely as if he were a modern psychologist writing plays, instead of novels. This is really what Mr Bradley does. He interprets Shakespeare from the psychological standpoint, but without once explaining what Shakespeare's psychology really was ; he *assumes* that it was like our own, but to do so is surely to throw Shakespeare out of the line of his historic development.

There *must have been* differences. What were they ? Not even a genius like Shakespeare can anticipate a method three centuries ahead of his own, and even if he had possessed such a truly outstanding gift of prophecy, we are only once more " up against " our main problem, the mentality of the audience ; his audience could not possibly have understood him.

The older editors of Shakespeare—Malone, for instance —do often see historical parallels. It was Coleridge who set the fashion of treating Shakespeare mainly from a psychological standpoint ; this was natural enough, for Coleridge was himself mainly a psychologist, and as he himself admits, possessed very little historic sense ; we may add that, in addition, there was very little historical material available. It is, however, somewhat surprising that, as the historical material became available, it was not more generally employed. Thus Mr Bradley (whom I quote so often, because he has carried this method to its farthest point), considers Shakespeare as almost entirely detached from his time and age ; the four great tragedies might almost have been written in the Age of Pericles or the period of the Romantic Revival for all the intimate and vital relation that Mr Bradley perceives between them and their own age.

But is this probable ?

We thus arrive at two very startling conclusions. One is that Shakespeare, though perhaps more interested in human nature than any man who has ever lived, wrote with almost complete indifference to his own era ; and this in spite of the fact that we know the Elizabethan stage was continually and closely associated with politics, and that Shakespeare's own company twice earned the displeasure of authority on account of Shakespeare's own plays, *two* [1] of which were certainly represented as having important political bearings.

The other is the equally startling conclusion that Shakespeare can be best interpreted by nineteenth-century psychology, not a sixteenth-century psychology (for that would probably have to be as obsolete as Ben Jonson's) ; but just precisely a nineteenth-century psychology.

Surely these results are very curious ?

But, it will be asked, if Shakespeare's greatest characters

[1] *Henry IV*. and *Richard II*.

are not predominantly psychological, in our sense of the term, what can they be ?

Let me take an illustration.

Suppose we consider again Shakespeare's Lear, and compare it with four allied characters, four characters who have much in common with him, choosing two from ancient, and two from modern literature. Suppose we compare Lear with Œdipus and Priam on the one side, and on the other, with Turgenieff's Lear of the Steppes, and Balzac's Père Goriot. With which group has Lear most in common ? To me it seems obvious that he has most in common with Œdipus and Priam. And Mr Bradley, when he compares *Lear* to the *Prometheus Vinctus*, is feeling the same effect that I feel. But Œdipus and Priam are characters in Greek mythology, whereas Turgenieff's Lear and Père Goriot are the characters of modern psychological realists.

Be it observed that it is not simply a question of genius, for the same hand which drew Lear also drew Nym, Pistol, and Bardolph ; but these latter belong quite plainly to the *Comedy of Humours*, they are psychology in the sixteenth-century (*i.e.* Jonsonian) sense of the term ; but they do not produce at all the same effect as Lear.

What, it may again be asked, is the essential difference between mythology and psychology ? Well, it seems to me that there are two differences which go to the root of the matter !

One is that the modern psychologist aims especially at the realistic portraits of *individuals*. He aims at giving you the sort of man you might meet anywhere, and this is what, when successful, he does. We all feel that

Turgenieff's Lear and Balzac's Père Goriot are individuals whom the authors might actually have met, and probably did meet. They are people of common life.

But do we feel that Œdipus and Priam are people of common life ?   On the contrary.   The poets wish to convey the impression that there is something in their heroes which is more than ordinary ; they are not merely ordinary individuals, they are something above and over. When Hermes visits Priam he compliments the old man on his great dignity and compares him to the immortal gods ; " divine Priam " is one of Homer's most constant epithets.

Now, if Hermes had ever met Lear he might have paid him the same compliment. Surely there is something exceptional and almost superhuman in the greatest figures of Shakespeare ? Do they produce the effect of being ordinary or even extraordinary *individuals* ? Does history record any man quite as pathetic as Lear, or quite as interesting as Hamlet ?   And even Lord Bacon does not seem as wise as Prospero.   Read his biography, and place it side by side with Shakespeare's Prospero, and see.

Has not Shakespeare himself hinted that his figures are partly mythologic and partly symbolic when he withdraws them so far from the everyday world. Why is Prospero placed in a magic island ?   Why are Hamlet and Macbeth and Lear all withdrawn into a remote and almost legendary past ?   Even Othello, who is much more like an ordinary human being, is still set apart as if he were a symbolic figure by his blackness.

The second great difference between the mythologist

and the psychologist is that the latter is not fundamentally historical, whereas the former is., The modern psychologist is pre-eminently an egoist and an individualist : he choses subjects mainly because they interest *him*, and all the importance they receive for others will be due to *his* method of treatment. In other words, as Hazlitt says of Wordsworth, he does not wish to share his own importance even with his subject. Flaubert, for instance, chooses in Madame Bovary an unimportant and almost trivial heroine ; all the interest is lent by *his* method of treatment.

The mythologist, on the other hand, deals with the matter which is traditional, which is a part of national history and which, as such, is already interesting to his audience as in the case of the Greek dramatists whose material is chosen from certain definite historic cycles.

Now, in this respect, Shakespeare and his fellows seem to offer a curious half-way house. Some of their subjects —such as Lear and Macbeth—are genuinely traditional in the Greek sense ; others—such as Othello—are derived from known sources but are not exactly traditional.

Now, if Shakespeare be truly a psychologic realist, it is exceedingly difficult to see why he did not invent his own plots. To economise labour is the usual reply—he took what was to hand to save himself trouble. Yes ! But the method which he actually did adopt was one which saved him no labour whatever, not, at least, in the majority of cases.

As anyone can see by comparing the two together, Shakespeare always reconstructs his source, and often alters it almost beyond recognition. In the case of Lear, for instance, the original story ended happily, so far, at any rate, as Lear himself was concerned ; the good daughter—Cordelia—restored him to his kingdom, and he reigned in peace until his death.

This is the version as we find it in practically all the Elizabethan sources ; Geoffrey of Monmouth, Holinshed, *The Mirror for Magistrates*, Spenser's *Faerie Queene*, etc., etc.

Moreover, in the original story, there was no Gloucester, no Edmund, no Edgar, all these figures come from a totally different source in Sidney's *Arcadia*, and they alter the whole bias of the plot. Why not recognise that the resulting story is really a new thing, and call it by a new name ?

Surely we find ourselves here on the horns of a very curious dilemma ! Does Shakespeare choose the subject of *King Lear*, as Coleridge says he did, because it was already endeared to the minds of his audience ? Quite possibly !

But, if so, why does he alter it so amazingly, for there is nothing, as a rule, which people more resent than an unfamiliar ending to a familiar tale ?

Moreover, Geoffrey of Monmouth's Lear does not strip himself entirely ; he retains a certain portion of his kingdom for himself, and it is to gain this portion that Goneril and Regan make war upon him. Thus, in the original tale, Lear, Goneril and Regan are all of them more intelligible in their actions than they are in Shakespeare. But why take an improbable plot, and then proceed to make it still more improbable by your method of treatment ?

The case is even more curious when we turn to compare *Hamlet* with its source.

In the original Amleth saga there is no ghost, no Polonius, no Ophelia, no Laertes ; the Polonius and Laertes story simply does not exist in the Amleth saga, and the ending is totally different, for the prince conquers his opponents, gets himself happily married to an English princess, and succeeds triumphantly to his father's throne. When he has killed his uncle he makes a speech to the assembled people : " It is I who have wiped off my country's shame ; I who have quenched my mother's dishonour ; I who have beaten back oppression ; I who have put to death the murderer ; I who have baffled the artful hand of my uncle with retorted arts. Were he living, each new day would have multiplied his crimes. I resented the wrong done to father and to fatherland : I slew him who was governing you outrageously, and more hardly than beseemed men. Acknowledge my service, honour my wit, give me the throne if I have earned it."

Amleth makes a long speech to this effect, and the conclusion of the whole matter is :

" Every heart had been moved while the young man thus spoke ; he affected some to compassion, and some even to tears. When the lamentation ceased, he was appointed king by general acclaim."

Moreover, the character of the hero is quite different for the hero of the Amleth saga never hesitates over his vengeance, but pursues it with undeviating energy. It is just because he does show such a magnificent combination of energy and subtlety that the people choose him as king. In fact, we should hardly know that *Hamlet* was supposed to be drawn from the Amleth saga, were it not for the similarity of the names, and for the fact, that, in each case, the hero is a Prince of Denmark.

Why retain the names when they mean so little ? Why not acknowledge that the story is new ?

In the case of *Hamlet*, at any rate, I shall endeavour to answer the question in the following pages.

I would sum up as follows :

(1) Shakespeare wrote his plays for a definite audience at a definite point of time. We know the period at which the plays were written, and we know, within a few years, the dates of the greater number. It should, therefore, be possible to discover with more or less accuracy what the plays would mean for their intended audience, and we cannot be sure that we comprehend them fully until we study the point of view of this audience.

(2) The point of view of an Elizabethan audience can only be understood by means of a careful study of the history of the time which should, therefore, be an integral part of the study of the plays.

(3) It is possible that we interpret Shakespeare too purely from a psychological standpoint ; in any case, the psychology of the sixteenth century is bound to differ from that of the nineteenth century, and it is important to show in what its differences consist.

I propose to apply this new method, as fully and as carefully as I can, in the case of *Hamlet*.

My one aim throughout will be to get the point of view of the Elizabethan audience and to make out, as far as

I can, what the play would mean to them, and what they would be likely to see in it.

I feel sure that the method is valid, though the results obtained from it certainly differ greatly from any of my own preconceived ideas.

CHAPTER I

RICHARD II. AND HAMLET

THE date of *Hamlet* is uncertain, but a careful examination of the evidence suggests that Shakespeare's first sketch of the play was written in 1601, and that this was expanded into the final form in 1603-4. It seems likely that Shakespeare wrote his first draft in 1601, while the Lord Chamberlain's men were travelling because they were for the time being out of favour at Court on account of their connection with the Essex conspiracy; this is apparently referred to in the allusion to the "inhibition of the players to perform in the city owing to the late innovation." [1]

The whole question of *Richard II.* is so closely bound up with that of *Hamlet*, that it is necessary to dwell upon it here at some length. It will show us, for one thing, how intimately Shakespeare's company and he himself were connected with political matters through the medium of Shakespeare's own plays, and it will show us also how material which might in itself seem innocent was regularly adapted to political purposes.

In the year 1596 the Pope published a bull empowering Elizabeth's own subjects to depose her. The queen knew that there was much discontent with her policy; Essex was an exceedingly popular and exceedingly gifted

---

[1] See Boas, *Shakespeare and His Predecessors.*

soldier, and his enemies insinuated to the queen that he aimed at deposing her, and seizing the crown for himself. Now Richard II. was a king who had been deposed, and the Essex partisans were suspected of using his fate as a kind of symbol of what Essex intended with Elizabeth. The queen and her advisers revealed continual nervousness on this subject.

On July 11th, 1600,[1] interrogations and notes were presented by Attorney-General Coke on Dr Haywarde's book on Richard II. in proof

" that the Doctor selected a story 200 years old and published it last year intending the application of it to this time, the plot being that of a king who is taxed for misgovernment and his counsel for corrupt and covetous dealings for private ends ; the king is censured for conferring benefits on hated favourites, the nobles become discontented and the commons groan under continual taxation, whereupon the king is deposed and in the end murdered."

Haywarde (it is stated) confessed that he had altered history in certain respects to suit his purposes ; as, for instance, having heard of a benevolence under Richard III. he transferred it to Richard II.

July 21st, 1600.   Essex admitted his treason.

"He permitted underhand that treasonable book of Henry IV. to be printed and published ; it being plainly deciphered, not only by the matter and by the epistle itself ; for what end and for whose behalf it was made, but also the Earl himself being so often present at the playing thereof[2] and with great applause giving countenance to it."

January 22nd, 1601.   The examination of Dr Haywarde showed how repeatedly he had altered his book.

[1] *Calendar of State Papers*, Green.
[2] This was, apparently, Shakespeare's play.

" Read in Bodires and other authors that the subject was bound to the state rather than to the person of the King ; inserted it as spoken by the Earl of Derby and Duke of Hereford to serve his own turn . . . did not invent the Earl's speech as it is, but found it somewhere. Set forth the oration of the Bishop of Canterbury according to matter found in other authorities and cannot affirm that he found these eight stories in any oration the Archbishop made ; but it is lawful for an historian so to do.

" Confesses that it is his own speech that it was not amiss in regard of the Commonwealth that King Richard II. was dead because it prevented civil war through two competitors . . . asked where he found the description of the Earl . . . says that he found in Hall and others that he was of popular behaviour, but for the particulars he took the liberty of the best writers.

" Gathered the description of the Earl out of his actions ; found the matter but not the form of the words."

Haywarde's book was dedicated to Essex in terms which in themselves suggested suspicions : the dedication ran :

" Roberto Comiti Essexiæ . . . Vicecomiti Herefordiæ " " cujus nomen si Henrici nostri fronte radiaret, ipse e latior et tutior in vulgus prodiret Magnus siquidem es et presenti judicio et futuri temporis expectatione : in quo, veluti re-cuperasse non oculos cæca prius fortuna videri potest."

The phrase about his future greatness was taken as referring to an expectation of the kingship.

The same book was referred to by Sir Robert Cecil, at the Essex trial, February 13th, 1601 [1] :

" He (*i.e.* Essex) conspired with Tyrone that Tyrone should land in England with an Irish army . . . these things ap-peared by the book written on Henry IV., making this time

---

[1] *State Papers*, Green.

seem like that of Richard II., to be by him as by Henry IV. deposed. . . . He would have removed her Majesty's servants, stepped into her chair and perhaps had her treated like Richard II."

And again :

" He came over from Ireland so unexpectedly to remove such from the Queen as he misliked, and could not bend to his traitorous faction ; then Tyrone and he were to join their forces and by destroying her Majesty Essex to be made King of England."

The same book is once more made important evidence against Essex in the " Directions to Preachers " given on February 14th :

" Two years since a history of Henry IV. was printed and published wherein all the complaints and slanders which have been given out by seditious traitors against the Government, both in England and Ireland, are set down and falsely attributed to those times, thereby cunningly insinuating that the same abuses being now in this realm that were in the days of Richard II., the like course might be taken for redress. . . .

" The Earl confessed that he kept the copy with him 14 days, plotting how he might become another Henry IV. . . .

" If he had not been prevented there had never been a rebellion in England since Richard II. more desperate and dangerous. . . ."

James Knowle said he had agreed with Tyrone that Tyrone should be king of Ireland and Essex of England.[1]

Now, Shakespeare's company were almost as much involved as Dr Haywarde in the dispute over Richard II., as is shown by the examination of Augustine Phillips (February 18th) ; Phillips is described as a servant to the Lord Chamberlain, and was therefore certainly a

[1] *State Papers*, Green.

member of Shakespeare's company.   "On Thursday or
Friday seven-night," runs the deposition,

"Sir Charles Percy, Sir Josceline Percy, Lord Mounteagle and
several others spoke to some of the players to play the
deposing and killing of King Richard and promised to give
them 40 shillings more than their ordinary to do so.

Examinate and his fellows had determined to play some
other play, holding that of King Richard as being so old and
so long out of use that they should have a small company at
it, but at this request they were content to play it."

Not only did they play it, but they went on playing it
some forty times in all during the whole period of the
trial and execution.   Wyndham says in this connection :

"Theatres were then, as newspapers are now, the cock-pits
of religious and literary contention. . . .

"The City Councillors could well, had they so minded, have
prevented the performance of *Richard II.*, with his deposition
and death some 'forty times' in open streets and houses, as
Elizabeth complained ; and indeed it is hard to account for
the Queen's sustained irritation at this drama save on the
ground of its close association with her past fears of Essex·
Months after the Earl's execution she exclaimed to Lambard :
'I am Richard the Second, know ye not that ? '

"Shakespeare's colleagues, acting Shakespeare's plays, gave
umbrage to Essex's political opponents in *Henry IV.*, applauded
his ambition in *Henry V.*, and were accessories to his dis-
loyalty in *Richard II.*" [1]

Shakespeare's company having incurred the serious displeasure of the queen, did not perform at Court, Christmas
1601–2, and it was during the period of their disgrace that,
according to Mr Boas,[2] *Hamlet* was most probably produced.

Three things become at once obvious when we consider
the above facts carefully.

[1] *Poems of Shakespeare.*
[2] *Shakespeare and His Predecessors.*

(1) That seemingly innocent subjects might be used, and, apparently, were often used, as in the case of Richard II., with a direct political bearing.

(2) That Shakespeare's company were twice accused [1] of using plays—*Henry IV., Richard II.*—for political purposes.

(3) That, in each case, the dramatic author involved was Shakespeare himself.

Now, what was the reply of Essex's friends to the accusation that he had intended to emulate Henry of Lancaster and make himself King of England? The answer was that Essex was an impassioned partisan of James I. and of the Scottish succession, and that he had fallen a martyr to the cause of James. Let us examine the political situation a little more closely in order to see how this came about. Let us endeavour to place ourselves in the exact position of an Elizabethan audience when the play of *Hamlet* was produced.

During the last years of Elizabeth's reign the great problem of practical politics lay in the succession to the throne. The queen was visibly growing feeble; she hated any mention of a successor; but it was obvious that, in the ordinary course of nature, her life could not last much longer. The Tudor policy had been to concentrate power in the hands of the monarchy, and, therefore, the character of the sovereign was all powerful in determining the future of the realm.

Foreign politics presented many points of extreme difficulty; Spain was still a most powerful and dangerous foe, continually plotting new Armadas: there was a plot

[1] See Introduction.

for a landing at Milford Haven in the very year of the queen's death, 1603.[1]

At no period in English history had the character of the monarch been more important, and in no single instance had the succession been so doubtful and men's minds so hopelessly distracted.

James of Scotland was, undoubtedly, the person who had the best title to the crown, but there were many reasons against him ; he had been set aside, somewhat unaccountably, by the will of Henry VIII. in favour of a younger branch ; he was a Scot, and, as such, might be considered ineligible ; by English law no Scottish subject could inherit landed property in England, not even the smallest estate ; how then, the lawyers argued, could a Scot inherit the throne ? [2]

There was also a considerable amount of prejudice against Scotland simply as a country.

" It is difficult," says Mr Martin Hume, " for Englishmen in these times to *conceive* the *distrust* and dislike then entertained for Scotchmen. They were, of course, foreigners and had for centuries been more or less closely allied to France, the secular enemy of England ; their country was poor and a large portion of it in semi-savagery." [3]

The Protestantism of Scotland was, naturally, a feature in its favour ; the English had vehemently taken the side of Murray and his Protestant lords as against the queen ; the English populace embraced the cause of Murray far more ardently than Elizabeth herself ; they espoused absolutely the cause of the Scottish lords, and when the

[1] Martin Hume, *Philip II.* (Cambridge Modern History, III.).
[2] Burton.
[3] *Sir Walter Ralegh.*

Scottish lords commissioned the historian—Buchanan—to defend their actions, the English populace probably accepted as accurate every word of his terrific indictment.

English sentiment was, on the whole, strongly in favour of James of Scotland ; he was the natural heir, and notwithstanding all prejudices against Scotland, there was an obvious and great advantage to be gained by uniting the whole island under one rule. The partisans of James very naturally pointed out the immense benefits that would accrue from the union of the crowns, and especially the great increase of safety to England herself.

It is worthy of note that those plays of Shakespeare which are obviously connected with Essex are also plays which all lay stress on the unity of Britain. Thus, in *Henry V.*, he pays an open and daring compliment to Essex,[1] then in Ireland, and it is also in *Henry V.* that he introduces, obviously as symbols of national unity, the four soldiers drawn from the four quarters of Britain : Gower the Englishman, Fluellen the Welshman, Macmorris the Irishman, and Jamy the Scotchman. This would be absurdly impossible in the time of the actual Henry V. ; but it represents the exact ideal at which the partisans of the Scottish succession were aiming when the play was written. The same thing may be said of the famous speech of the dying John of Gaunt in *Richard II.* :

> " This royal throne of kings, this scepter'd isle
> .   .   .   .   .   .
> This fortress built by Nature for herself
> Against infection and the hand of war."

English sentiment was, for these reasons, strongly in

[1] Act V., Chorus.

favour of James of Scotland ; but it could not be said to be unanimous ; there were the legal difficulties in the way, and a further difficulty lay in the character of James himself.

James' character had, or seemed to have, many admirable traits ; but it was a baffling and a difficult one. He had a great reputation for learning, and for interest in philosophy and theology ; he was mild and merciful by temperament, sternness and cruelty were far from him ; he hated bloodshed, and he was the least revengeful of men ; no trait in him was more marked than his reluctance to punish even when punishment seemed just and necessary, and most of the odium he incurred in life was on account of this very reluctance. His whole tone of mind was serious and reflective, and, though he was often coarse in his language, he was exempt from the grosser vices.

On the other hand, he was totally unlike the Tudor sovereigns with their love of pleasure, their *bonhomie*, their frank willingness to mingle with all classes of their subjects. He was melancholy and retiring ; he had one confidant in the Earl of Mar, his fellow-pupil under Buchanan—in whom he seemed to repose implicit trust ; but to the majority of men he was inaccessible and difficult. He loved seclusion in a way almost incomprehensible to people accustomed to the bustling and vigorous temperament of the Tudors.

His political position was, and always had been, one of extraordinary difficulty ; with his father murdered, his mother in lifelong imprisonment, and his country full of factious, partisan nobles, there seems to have been no one, except possibly Mar, whom he could intimately trust.   His weapons in these circumstances were a baffling subtlety, a habit of verbal fence, a passion for keeping his own counsel which went so far that he was at times suspected of insanity.   His position made him a very close student of men and manners, for his very existence depended on the care and accuracy of his judgment ; almost all his Stuart predecessors had met premature deaths, several by assassination, and he only escaped a similar fate by his reticence and subtlety, his genius for evasion.   All his life he prided himself on his knowledge of human nature, his power of judging character at a glance, and so far as his youth was concerned, he had apparently exercised that knowledge with considerable skill ; at any rate he preserved himself from a premature death which was more than any of his Stuart predecessors had done.

His melancholy, his love of seclusion, his baffling subtlety, the occasional doubts of his sanity might all be explained by the difficulties of his position, and by the shifts to which he was put in extricating himself from such serious perils.

His extraordinary carelessness and untidiness in dress, which revolted many observers, might possibly be set down to a similar cause.

More serious defects, however, suggested themselves, the most fatal being, apparently, a singular vacillation and weakness of will.   The Tudors had been, above all, strong and vigorous statesmen ;   they were powerful rulers ;   their will-power and determination ranked with their popularity among their chief assets.   But James seemed incapable of strong and effective action ;   he allowed the younger Bothwell to usurp power and practically make himself the master of Scotland while he, James, stood aside in comparative retirement; the younger Bothwell held him in a kind of *duresse vile*, and James made no effective protest.

Anyone who will read the correspondence of Elizabeth and James will see how continually the queen reproaches him for these defects of character; he knows very well, she maintains, that his subjects destroy his royal authority, and even plot against his life; but he does not execute justice. It is right to be merciful; but when mercy shows itself as complaisance towards villains and scoundrels, then mercy itself becomes a weakness.

It is his duty as a king to defend his realm against evil doers, to execute justice, and to punish rebels; his realm is a mass of disorder; it proceeds from bad to worse, and it is his fault because he does not punish where punishment is due. So long as violence is allowed to flourish, there can be no security in a kingdom. Elizabeth reiterates these charges again and again, in different epistles and in various ways. And James hardly defends himself. He practically admits that the indictment is just; he sees what he ought to do, but he cannot do it; he knows very well that the times are out of joint, but he does not feel himself vigorous enough to set them right; he cannot assume the necessary severity. The queen accuses him continually of vacillation and delay; he knows what he ought to do, why does he not do it? And James can only reply by admitting the procrastination and acknowledging the delay. From the Tudor point of view, this vacillation of will and this procrastination were precisely the qualities most dangerous to a monarch and most likely to be fatal to his people.

We, in these later days, inevitably consider James I. and VI. from what we know of his history on the English throne ; it is prosperity, as Bacon says, which really tries a man ; but the James who was known to the Elizabethans in the year 1601 was almost precisely the James described above ; there is not a single trait which has not complete warrant in the Scottish historians or in his own correspondence with Elizabeth.[1]

We must also remember the fact that the Scottish monarch had a special connection with Denmark ; his queen—Anne—was a princess of Denmark ; he himself had brought her home in a romantic voyage ; there were Danes resident at the Scottish court.   Moreover, the murderer of James' father, the elder Bothwell, had also taken refuge in Denmark and had ended his life imprisoned there.

This, then, was the political situation at the exact moment *Hamlet* was written : the whole future of the realm turned on the question of the succession and the character of the future monarch ; the most direct heir to the realm was a prince who was melancholy by temperament, whose character seemed flawed by a vacillating will and a habit of procrastination ; on the other hand, he had an unexpected capacity for acting with decision in emergencies, as, for instance, in the Gowry conspiracy ; he was one of the most learned princes in Europe, and he took an intense interest in philosophy and theology.

[1] See especially Burton and Hume Brown.

His whole situation was tragic and difficult : his father had been murdered, and his mother had married the murderer ; to the amazement of Europe he had allowed his royal authority to be usurped and his own person placed in jeopardy by a man of the same title and family as the usurper, a person who, to the excited imagination of the time, seemed almost like a reincarnation of the same evil genius who had ruined the mother.

Let us now examine carefully the connection of Shakespeare's friends and patrons with the Scottish prince. The nation, taken as a whole, seems to have profoundly mistrusted the Cecils, and Essex made himself the mouthpiece of this mistrust. It was known how completely Elizabeth trusted Burleigh and how great her confidence was ; but the Essex faction accused him of dishonest diplomacy, of spying, of eavesdropping, of " laying trains to entrap people " and many other objectionable practices. After the death of Burleigh Robert Cecil succeeded, and more than succeeded, to his father's ill-repute. One group of his enemies accused him of designing to marry the Lady Arabella Stuart, and seize the crown for himself in her name ; Essex, at his trial, declared that Robert Cecil was in collusion with the Spaniards and wished to deliver the crown to the Spanish Infanta ; it is quite possible that Essex sincerely believed this, and that it was one of the motives for his action—at any rate, he said so upon his oath.

It is obvious that the Essex conspiracy was aimed especially at Raleigh and Robert Cecil, and was essentially an endeavour to take the queen from their influence.

With the details of this conspiracy, in so far as they affect Shakespeare, I will deal later. Here I only wish to point out that Shakespeare himself had a double connection with it, once through his company and once through his friend and patron—Southampton.

The Essex conspirators had, as we have seen, requested Shakespeare's company to perform the play of *Richard II.*, since, because it dealt with the deposition of a monarch, it was supposed to have a definite bearing on their case.

The attempt on the queen's person was made and failed; Essex, the brilliant idol of the populace, was tried and executed; Southampton, Shakespeare's patron and friend, was condemned to death, though afterwards reprieved, and at the time *Hamlet* was written he was still in the Tower.

Shakespeare's company, as we have seen, were practically disgraced because of their sympathy with Essex. So general was this sympathy and so determined were the players to make capital of it on the stage, that for several years after the Essex conspiracy no plays dealing with any conspiracy were allowed at all, the authorities being firmly convinced that any conspiracy play, whatever its ostensible subject, would really allude to Essex.

Now, in addition to these reasons—the popular sympathy with Essex, his own company's marked connection—Shakespeare had reasons of his own for taking the greatest interest in the Essex conspiracy. Southampton was certainly Shakespeare's most generous patron; if, as seems plausible, he was also the hero of the sonnets, he was Shakespeare's best-beloved friend. As the result of his connection with that conspiracy he was under sentence of death ; he was reprieved for the time being ; but, any day, the intrigues of Robert Cecil and his faction might destroy him.

Such was the exact situation when Shakespeare's *Hamlet* was produced.

CHAPTER II

HAMLET AND THE DARNLEY MURDER

THE subject of *Hamlet* was sufficiently well known before Shakespeare treated of it. It is told in the *Historia Danica* of Saxo Grammaticus, who wrote about 1180–1208. It appeared translated into French in Belleforest's *Histoires Tragiques* in 1570. There is an English prose version, *The Hystorie of Hamblet*, which dates from 1608 and is thus certainly later in date than the play, though possibly there were earlier versions which have been lost.

There can be no doubt that a play on the subject existed as early as 1589, for Nash makes a plain reference to it in his preface to Greene's *Menaphon* (1587 or 1589), and Lodge in his *Wit's Miserie* alludes to a ghost which cried like an oyster-wife, "Hamlet, revenge ": *a* play of *Hamlet* was also performed by the Lord Chamberlain's company in 1594. There is a general consensus of opinion that this early *Hamlet cannot* have been by Shakespeare, since Meres does not refer to it in his famous list given in the *Palladis Tamia* of 1598.

The general consensus of opinion is that this early drama was probably by Kyd.

Since Kyd's play has disappeared, it is totally impossible to ascertain whether he did or did not use historical material as an element in that drama though, so far as concerns any material existing previous to 1589, he may quite well have done so, and I would call the reader's attention very carefully to the fact, for it may be significant, that the only historical parallels I find to *known* elements in the earlier *Hamlet* are all, as a matter of fact, anterior to this date. My method will be to compare the play with the *Amleth* story on the one side and the historical details on the other, and to show that the action of the play far more closely agrees with that of history than with that of the saga, and also that the main problems of the play are not the problems of the saga but are certainly those of the history.

In Shakespeare's drama the queen is called Gertrude ; her first husband is Hamlet, like his son, and the murderous usurper is Claudius. In the saga, the queen is Geruth, her first husband is Horvendil, and his brother, who slays him, is Feng.

What the saga says concerning the murder is the following :

" Such great good fortune stung Feng with jealousy so that he resolved treacherously to waylay his brother—thus showing that goodness is not safe even from those of a man's own household. And behold, when a chance came to murder him, his bloody hand sated even the deadly passion of his soul. Then he took the wife of the brother he had butchered, capping unnatural murder with incest."

Feng admits his brother's murder to the people ; but he invents a justification for his deed by saying that his brother had planned the murder of the queen— Gertrude. There was thus nothing secret about the murder which took place publicly, and which was acknowledged before the whole court. The prose *Hystorie*

D

of Hamblet gives exactly the same version as Saxo Grammaticus; it tells how the adulterer murdered his brother at a banquet, and then slandered the dead man by saying that he would have slain his wife; "so, instead of pursuing him as a parricide and an incestuous person, all the courtiers admired and flattered him in his good fortune."

We may now turn to Shakespeare and note how close are the known parallels to the history of James I.—the identical person in whom both Shakespeare and his audience had, at that moment, reason to take such a profound interest.

To begin with, the device of having the murder told by a ghost has no parallel whatever in the saga source (there would be no motive for it); but it had a parallel in the Darnley murder for the Scottish ballad-makers had already hit on exactly that device. Thus, in Edinburgh, 1567, there was published a ballad entitled *The Testament and Tragedie of the umquhile King Henrie Stuart, of gude memorie.*

In it, the unhappy ghost of the murdered king returns and laments:

> " Sum tyme scho [1] thocht I was sa amiabill,
> Sa perfect, plesand, and sa delectabill;
> . . . she luid me by all wycht;
> Sum tyme, to show affectioun favourabill,
> Gratifeit me with giftis honorabill;
>   .   .   .   .   .
> Sum tyme in mynde she praisit me sa hycht
> Leifand all uther; hir bedfellow brycht
> Chesit me to be and maid me your king."

---

[1] *i.e.* Mary.

Then, further, the murder in the saga takes place, as we have seen, in an open and obvious way, and is fully acknowledged.

In Shakespeare the ghost explains that his murder is secret and stealthy [1]:

> " Now, Hamlet, hear :
> 'Tis given out that, sleeping in my orchard,
> A serpent stung me ; so the whole ear of Denmark
> Is by a forged process of my death
> Rankly abused :
> . . . Sleeping within my orchard,
> My custom always of the afternoon,
> Upon my secure hour thy uncle stole
> With juice of cursed hebenon in a vial,
> And in the porches of my ears did pour
> The leporous distilment ; . . .
> And a most instant tetter bark'd about,
> Most lazar-like, with vile and loathsome crust,
> All my smooth body."

Now, the father of James 1. was finally murdered by means of, or at least concurrently with, a gunpowder explosion ; but it was very generally believed that a previous attempt had been made to poison him.

Burton [2] says :

" Darnley was seized with a sudden and acute illness which broke out cutaneously. Poison was at first naturally suspected. The disease was speedily pronounced to be small-pox ; but it has been conjectured that it may have been one of those forms of contamination which had then begun to make their silent and mysterious visitation in this country, while the immediate cause by which they were communicated was yet unknown. From what occurred afterwards it became a current belief that he had been poisoned."

---

[1] Act I., v.   [2] *History of Scotland,* Vol. IV.

The plot for his destruction with gunpowder was next attempted; but it does not appear that he perished as a result of the explosion. Burton continues:

> " It seems that the intended victim with his page . . . attempted to escape and even got over a wall into a garden when they were seized and strangled. They were found without any marks from the explosion but with marks of other violence."

Now here we surely have remarkable correspondences with the Shakespearian murder: we have the body of the victim covered with a " loathsome tetter " which is ascribed to the malign influence of poison ; we have the secret character of the murder itself, and we have the body of the victim found in an " orchard."

Let us once again compare Shakespeare with a source which was certainly available both for himself and for his audience, Buchanan's *Detection*.[1]

> " Ere he was passed a mile from Stirling all the parts of his body were taken with such a sore ache, as it might easily appear that the same proceeded not of the force of any sickness but by plain treachery. The tokens of which treachery, certain black pimples, so soon as he was come to Glasgow, broke out all over his whole body with so great ache and such pain throughout his limbs, that he lingered out his life with very small hope of escape ; and yet all this while the queen would not suffer so much as a physician to come near him."

Buchanan dwells on the same theme in his *Oration*,[2] also a source available alike to Shakespeare and Shakespeare's audience, and probably known very well to all of them :

> " It is certainly known that he was poisoned. . . . For

---

[1] Scotch Version, 1572.
[2] Possibly by another hand.

though the Shamelessness of Men would not stick to deny a thing so manifest ; yet the kind of Disease, strange, unknown to the People, unacquainted with Physicians, especially such as had not been in Italy and Spain, black Pimples breaking out all over his body, grievous aches in all his limbs and intolerable stink disclosed it—there is no Adulteress but the same is also a Poisoner. Read her own Letter. He is not much deformed and yet he hath received much. Whereof hath he received much ? The thing itself, the Disease, the Pimples, the Savor do tell you. Even that much he received that brought Deformity, Forsooth, very Poison. Whatsoever it was that he received the same, the same was the Cause of his Deformity.

" . . . She will have the manner of ministring the Medicine to be secret. If it be to heal him what needs that secrecy ? . . . To whom is this Charge committed to seek out a new Medicine and curing for the King ? Forsooth to the King's Enemy, to the Queen's adulterer, the vilest of all two-footed beasts, whose house was in France defamed for poisoning and whose Servants were there for the same cause, some tortured, some imprisoned, and all suspected. . . .

" So forsooth are Medicines accustomed to be provided by Enemies, in a secret Place, without Witnesses. That therefore which an Adulterer and Adulteress, and the partner of the Wife's Body, curiously prepareth and secretly ministreth ; what Medicine this is, let every Man with himself weigh and consider."

We see here the immense stress which Buchanan lays on the *secrecy* of the murder, on the solitude of the unhappy victim at the time the poisoning took place, on the foulness produced in his body, the deformity, the pustules, etc., all of which agree closely with the murder of Hamlet's father, and, what is especially significant, not *one* of these details is to be found in either of the prose versions. In the so-called literary source, the murder is *not* secret, the victim is *not* alone, poison is *not* used, deformity is *not* caused. It is worthy of note that the very term the ghost uses in describing his condition, "leprous," had been applied by contemporary writers to Darnley.

A satirist called him "the leper," leprosy being confounded with "la grosse verole." [1]

We may also observe that Buchanan insists that the method of poisoning was well known in France and Italy, and Hamlet himself compares his father's death to the Italian murder of Gonzago.

Buchanan says : "There is no adulteress but the same is also a poisoner," and Hamlet has : "None wed the second but who killed the first." [2]

We may compare also Buchanan's own satire appended to his Latin version :

> "Et quem non potuit morientem auferre veneno
> Hunc fera, sulphureo pulvere tollit humo,
>
> .   .   .   .
>
> Nobilis ille tuas vires Darnleuis heros
> pertulit, heu tristes pertulit ille faces.
>
> .   .   .   .
>
> Siccine Bothwellum poteras sine lege tenere ?
> Siccine Bothwelli poterant te flectere verba."

This, again, has a close resemblance to the ghost's lament :

> "Ay, that incestuous, that adulterate beast,
> With witchcraft of his wit.
> O wicked wit and gifts that have the power
> So to seduce."

Buchanan terms Bothwell "an adulterer," and "the

---

[1] Andrew Lang, *Mystery of Mary Stuart*.   [2] Act III., ii.

vilest of all two-legged beasts," who has power to bend the queen with his words, and Shakespeare uses almost the same phrases.

Another curious detail of the murder may be observed here. The ghost declares that he was murdered by poison—henbane—poured *in his ear* while he slept. Now, Mary's accusers,[1] to heap calumny upon her, had accused her of conniving also at the murder of her first husband—Francis II. of France. That unhappy prince died from an abscess *in the ear*, but it was a common rumour that it was caused by poison inserted *in the ear*.

Now, does it not look as if Shakespeare were combining in one most powerful and dramatic scene these three attempts all associated with Mary Queen of Scots : the poison in the ear from the reputed murder of Francis II., the loathsomeness and vileness of the unhappy victim from the first attempt on Darnley, and the body of the victim found in the garden with the actual murder of Darnley? Why not? All these three attempts had already been associated together, one strengthening another, by the queen's accusers,[2] and a dramatic poet very naturally desires to make his play as intense and moving as he can. The association, like the Darnley ghost, is already there. Why not use it ?

There is, however, one important modification. At the time when Mary Queen of Scots was executed, she was regarded by the people of England with embittered hate, and it is more than probable that every word of Buchanan's

---

[1] See Leslie, Bishop of Ross (*Hatfield Papers*).
[2] See Leslie, Bishop of Ross.

terrific indictment was regarded as true. James had, however, a certain respect for the memory of his mother, and it is probable that anyone who desired to please him might be inclined to take a lenient view of Mary's connection with the crime. It has been possible even for modern historians to deny altogether or in part her connection with it, and her apologists of course (like Belleforest) did so in Shakespeare's own time.

Now, this is very much what happens in *Hamlet*. In the saga there is no doubt whatever as to the queen's guilt ; she has not only committed adultery, she has connived at the murder, and acquiesced in the false statement invented to justify the deed. In Shakespeare, on the contrary, we have the subtlety and complexity of the history—nothing whatever is said to make it plain that the queen has knowingly acquiesced in her husband's murder. She may have done ; but though the ghost accuses her of adultery he does not say that she connived at the other crime. His attitude towards her is always tender and indulgent, and Darnley, we may remember, to the last day of his recorded life sought the love of Mary, and pathetically believed in the possibility of a reconciliation with her. That is half the pathos of Darnley's fate, and it is certainly half the pathos of Shakespeare's ghost that he continues to love his erring wife in spite of all.

As a reference to Buchanan will at once show, he lays enormous stress on the undiminished affection of the unhappy victim which survived even the attempt to poison him. " Why," asks Buchanan,[1] " did she thrust

[1] *Oration.*

away from her the young Gentleman . . . he being
beautiful, near of her kin, of the Blood Royal and (that
which is greatest), most entirely loving her."

Again, both the ghost and Hamlet call attention to
the fickleness of the queen. The ghost claims that he
won her swiftly : he says his love

> " was of that dignity
> That it went hand in hand even with the vow
> I made to her in marriage."

This, again, looks as if it were suggested by the rapid
marriage of Mary and Darnley after a brief acquaintance.

Again, even before he has seen the ghost, Hamlet
dwells on the fact that his mother used to show such
an intense affection for his father ; but forgot him so
soon and declined upon one whose gifts were so far
inferior.

> " Heaven and earth !
> Must I remember ? why, she would hang on him,
> As if increase of appetite had grown
> By what it fed on : and yet, with a month—
> . . . married with my uncle,
> My father's brother, but no more like my father
> Than I to Hercules . . .
> O most wicked speed, to post,
> With such dexterity to incestuous sheets." [1]

Now, this is precisely one of Buchanan's chief indict-
ments against Mary, that she so vehemently loved her
first husband, but so rapidly forgot him and married the
second who was so immeasurably his inferior in person
and charm.

[1] Act I., ii.

These are some of the most apposite passages :

" What if I ask again why she so extremely loved the young
Man ? why she so hastily married him and so unmeasur-
able honoured him ?   Such are the natures of some
women.

" That husband therefore whom she lately wedded . . .
without whom she could not endure, whom she scarcely
durst suffer out of her sight, him she thrust forth."

" . . . that adulterous partner, neither in birth nor in
beauty nor in any honest quality was in any wise comparable
with her disdained husband."

" Bothwell was an Ape in purple."

" Neither is the cause unknown why she did it. Even
that the same filthy marriage with Bothwell might be
accomplished."

" One is divorced, another is coupled, and that in such
posting speed, as they might have scant have hasted to
furnish any triumph of some noble victory." [1]

Here, again, we have phrases which closely resemble
Shakespeare's " posting to incestuous sheets."

Both Hamlet and the ghost lay enormous stress on this
indecent haste, and on the contrast between the two
husbands :

" A little month, or ere those shoes were old
With which she follow'd my poor father's body,
Like Niobe, all tears :—why she, even she,—
O God ! a beast that wants discourse of reason
Would have mourned longer . . .
                    within a month
Ere yet the salt of most unrighteous tears
Had left the flushing in her galled eyes."

We may observe also that this hasty marriage was
held from the beginning to affect closely James himself.

[1] *Oration.*   Scotch version.

Burton quotes from the memoirs of Sir James Melville :

" every good subject that loved the queen's honour and the prince's security had sad hearts and thought her majesty would be dishonoured and the prince in danger to be cut off by him who had slain his father."

Now here, again, we have the atmosphere of Hamlet : the queen's disgraceful haste, the secrecy and suspicion and the peril of her son.

Buchanan says [1] :

" When of the forty days appointed for the mourning, scarce twelve were yet fully past . . . taking heart of grace unto her, and neglecting such trifles, she cometh to her own bias, and openly sheweth her own natural conditions."

Buchanan dwells on the fact that before the marriage, Bothwell was accused of having committed fornication with his wife's own kinswoman . . . and the divorce with Lady Jane Bothwell was " posted forward."

" And so at length within the eight days (from the time of the divorce commenced), she finished that unmatrimonial matrimony, all good men so far detesting or at least grudgingly forejudging the unlucky end thereof.

" . . . but Monsieur de Croce though he was earnestly desired could not with his honour be present at the feast."

Buchanan makes out Bothwell to be a kind of specialist in adultery : " Bothwell had then alive two wives already, not yet divorced and the third neither lawfully married nor orderly divorced."

" The deed," says Buchanan, " of itself is odious in a woman, it is monstrous in a wife, not only excessively loved but also most zealously honoured, it is incredible. And

---

[1] *Detection.*

being committed against him . . . whose affection requires love . . . upon that young man in whom there is not so much as alleged any just cause of offence."

Here, again, we may remember what Hamlet says of his father's affection for his mother :

> " he might not beteem the winds of heaven
> Visit her face too roughly."

Throughout Shakespeare's drama enormous stress is laid on the difference in character and appearance between the two husbands. Now almc t all the contemporary records stress this difference in the case of Darnley and Bothwell.

" He (*i.e.* Darnley) was a comely Prince of a fair and large stature of body, pleasant in countenance, affable to all men and devout, well-exercised in martial pastimes upon horse-back as any prince of that age." [1]

Compare Horatio's address to the ghost,[2]

> " What art thou that usurp'st this time of night,
> Together with that fair and warlike form
> In which the majesty of buried Denmark
> Did sometimes march ? "

And also the description of Marcellus :

> " With martial stalk hath he gone by our watch."

In 1566 de Silva learned from Mauvissière that he (Darnley) mostly passed his time in warlike exercises, and was a good horseman. Causin speaks of him as " being accomplished with all excellent endowments both of body and of mind." [3]

---

[1] *Historie of James the Sixt.*   [2] Act I., i.
[3] Quoted by Hay Fleming.

Knox's continuator thus describes him : " He was of a comely stature and none was like unto him within this island."

Buchanan says in his *Detection* (of Mary): " She long beheld . . . with greedy eyes his dead corpse, the goodliest corpse of any gentleman that ever lived in this age."

Compare this with Horatio's speech : [1]

> " I saw him once ; he was a goodly king,"

and Hamlet's reply :

> " He was a man, take him for all in all,
> I shall not look upon his like again."

Again we note as somewhat curious the immense stress that is laid upon the armour of the ghost ; it makes him more dignified and more warlike. So, also, Darnley had a fancy for appearing in full armour which some persons thought an affectation, and which his enemies ridiculed ; thus in 1565 he appeared in full armour at Mary's side in their brief war against the Lords of the Congregation ; it was, in that age at any rate, a real peculiarity.

Bothwell, on the other hand, is persistently described by Buchanan and others as a needy adventurer, given to vices of a low cast : drunkenness and licentiousness.

Buchanan says :

" What was there in him Bothwell that was of a woman of any honest countenance to be desired, was there any gift of eloquence or grace of beauty or virtue of mynd. . . .

---

[1] Act I., ii.

As for his eloquence we need not speak . . . they that have heard him are not ignorant of his rude utterance and blockishness . . . his enemies face he never durst abide . . . by a thief, a notable coward, he was deadly wounded and thrown to the ground. . . . He was brought up in the Bishop of Murray's palace . . . in drunkenness and whoredoms, among vile ministries of dissolute misorder. . . . Bothwell was a man in extreme poverty, doubtful whether he were more vile or more wicked. . . . As for excessive and immoderate use of lechery, he therein no less sought to be famous than other men do shun dishonour and infamy."

We have thus in Bothwell exactly the same type of character as that depicted in Claudius : Hamlet alludes with emphatic disgust to the heavy drinking of the king, he dwells on his licentiousness and points the bitter contrast between Claudius and his brother, exactly as Buchanan points the contrast between the hideousness and licentiousness of Bothwell and the beauty and stateliness of Darnley (Acts III.–IV.).

> " See, what a grace was seated on this brow ;
> Hyperion's curls, the front of Jove himself, . . .
> This was your husband.   Look you now, what
>   follows ;
> Here *is* your husband ; like a mildewed ear
> Blasting his wholesome brother. . . .
>   Ha ! have you eyes ?
> You cannot call it love."

So Buchanan insists that the passion of Mary for Bothwell cannot properly have been called love, but only that insensate rage of lust which sometimes seizes upon women and blinds them to all that is base in character and hideous in person.

Hamlet accuses Claudius [1] of exactly the vices condemned in Bothwell : he speaks of killing him

> " When he is drunk asleep, or in his rage
> Or in the incestuous pleasure of his bed,
> At gaming, swearing or about some act
> That has no relish of salvation in't."

His drunkenness, of course, and its corrupting effect on the court is insisted on from the very beginning [2] : Hamlet says to Horatio :

> " what is your affair in Elsinore ?
> We'll teach you to drink deep ere you depart."

Bothwell's enemies had accused him of practising art magic, and both Mary's friends and enemies, including the hostile lords in their proclamations, averred that Bothwell had won her favour by unlawful means, philtres, witchcraft, or what we may call hypnotism.

Shakespeare does not represent Hamlet as accusing Claudius of the Black Art, but he may be referring to these accusations when he makes the ghost accuse him of seducing the queen " with witchcraft of his wicked wit."

I have already pointed out,[3] that in *Hamlet* the ghost is a Catholic, whereas his son is a Protestant, and this is another matter in which the play differs totally from the saga and corresponds closely with the history.

Horatio, in the opening of the play,[4] has just come

---

[1] Act III., iii.   [2] Act I., ii.
[3] Introduction.   [4] Act I., ii.

from Wittenberg, and Hamlet greets him as his " fellow-student " ; Hamlet also desires to return to Wittenberg, which Claudius does not wish to permit.

> " For your intent
> In going back to school in Wittenberg
> It is most retrograde to our desire." [1]

Nothing, of course, is said of any Wittenberg in the saga, and I am positive that any reader who cares to refer to Saxo Grammaticus will feel that the mention of any modern university would be singularly out of place in that barbarous production.

But Wittenberg, on account of its association with Luther, was famous as one of the chief Protestant centres of Europe ; Scottish universities, as already pointed out, had in the sixteenth century a very close and intimate connection with German Protestant universities, and thus the mention of Wittenberg certainly suggests a Protestant connection for both Horatio and Hamlet.

It is equally clear that the ghost is Catholic. He speaks of purgatory, and of himself as being condemned to its penalties [2] :

> " Doom'd for a certain time to walk the night,
> And for the day confined to fast in fires,
> Till the foul crimes done in my days of nature
> Are burnt and purged away : "

The ghost, be it noted, lays no claim to entire innocence of life ; he admits " foul crimes." In the whole cruel and bitter story of his murder the thing that grieves him

[1] Act I., ii.   [2] Act I., v.

most is that he had no opportunity for absolution and extreme unction.

> " Cut off even in the blossoms of my sin,
> Unhousel'd, disappointed, unaneled,
> No reckoning made, but sent to my account
> With all my imperfections on my head ;
> O horrible ! O horrible ! most horrible ! "

Now here, again, we have an exact parallel with the history ; Darnley was a Catholic, he had committed " foul crimes," and he was cut off without the possibility of absolution and extreme unction. The son, James I., was a Protestant and a very keen and eager student, a fact on which he greatly plumed himself, of Protestant theology.

In the saga story there is, of course, no ghost. Its function would, indeed, be totally unnecessary as neither Amleth nor anyone else has the least doubt as to the guilt of the king, who, as we have seen, acknowledged it.

In the history, however, tne guilt of the culprits certainly was doubtful ; Bothwell seized the supreme power ; he was not at first openly accused, but suspicions were rife against him. Burton says : " Those who dared not speak openly gave utterance in the dark, and midnight accusations were heard with mysterious awe. Sir William Drury tells Cecil of a man who went about crying : ' Vengeance on those who . . . caused the shedding of innocent blood. O Lord ! open the heavens and pour down vengeance.' " [1]

[1] *History of Scotland.*

E

Buchanan alludes to the same thing : people dared not openly accuse Bothwell of the offence,

" specially as he himself was doer, judge, enquirer and examiner. Yet this fear which stopped the mouths of every man in particular could not restrain the multitude. Because both by books set out, by pictures and by cries in the dark night, it was so set out and handled that the doers of the mischievous fact might easily understand that those secrets of theirs were come abroad."

Buchanan has also a curious tale of an apparition which came to the Earl of Athol and three of his friends on the night of the Darnley murder, wakened them out of their sleep, and apprised them of the crime.

As we have also seen, there was a contemporary ballad which represented the ghost of Darnley as returning to tell his own pitiful tale.

In the original prose story there was no voice crying out murder in the night and no apparition ; Shakespeare seems to have put them together, and dramatised them into the truly magnificent conception of the ghost of Hamlet's father.

There was certainly a ghost in the earlier Hamlet —the play ascribed to Kyd—but, as I have already remarked, we have no means of knowing whether Kyd was using historical sources or not.

Other curious details in the ghost-scene are worthy of comment. Thus the ghost tells Hamlet that it is compelled to depart ; but, when Hamlet exacts the oath of silence from Horatio and the soldiers, the ghost reappears in the most extraordinary way *beneath* the ground, so that Hamlet refers to him as " this fellow in the cellarage " and calls him " an old mole."

Now it was the murder of Rizzio which steeled Mary's heart against her husband, and it was very generally believed that Mary took an oath to murder him over Rizzio's grave. The Lennox MSS. are the main authorities for this incident; they aver that, when Darnley and Mary were escaping together through the vaults of Holyrood, Darnley paused and uttered remorseful words over Rizzio's new-made grave; they aver that Mary, seeing the grave, said " it should go very hard with her but a fatter than Rizzio should lie anear him ere one twelvemonth was at an end." Moreover, on the evening preceding Darnley's death, Mary is said to have reminded him of this very incident :

" Rizzio," says Mr Andrew Lang, " was buried in the chapel vaults. In their escape Mary and Darnley passed by his grave ; she is said to have declared that ' ere a year he should have a fatter by his side !' On the evening preceding Darnley's death she reminded him that it was a year since Rizzio's murder." [1]

Martin Hume speaks of the pretended reconciliation of the husband and wife :

" In the course of their loving talk Mary dropped a sinister hint that just a year had passed since Rizzio's murder ; and, when she had gone, Darnley in the hearing of his pages, expressed his uneasiness that she had recollected it, for he at least had not forgotten her threat over Rizzio's grave." [2]

Buchanan [3] says :

" One Sunday night she discovered herself, and fetching a deep sigh : ' O says she, this time twelve month was David

---

[1] *Mystery of Mary Stuart.*
[2] *Love Affairs of Mary Stuart.*
[3] *Detection.*

Rizzio slain.'   This it seems came from her heart ; for within a few days, the unfortunate young Man, as an Inferiæ to the Ghost of a Fidler, was strangled in his Bed . . . and his Body thrown out into the garden"; and again "suddenly, without any Funeral Honour in the Night Time, by common Carriers of dead Bodies, upon a vile Bier, she caused him to be buried by David Rizzio."

It was thus a definite belief of Shakespeare's age, as the quotations above clearly show, that the oath ensuring the murder of Darnley had been taken in the vaults of Holyrood over the grave of Rizzio, and that this oath was punctually and to the time fulfilled.

Does it not look as if it were this that had suggested the scene when the ghost in his turn reminds Hamlet of *his* oath with the voice that comes from the "Cellarage." The whole incident was, to the last degree, gruesome and suggestive, and is it not most exceedingly plausible that a popular dramatist and a tragic dramatist would prefer to work upon the emotions that he knew to be existing in the minds of his audience ?   This is why we cannot be assured that we understand Shakespeare fully unless we take into account the Elizabethan point of view, for the associations existing in their minds, and to which the dramatist would naturally appeal, do not exist in ours.

Another resemblance to the Darnley murder lies in the attitude of the queen who is always loyal to her second husband ; she will not leave him even for Hamlet's bitter rebukes, and she takes his part until the end.

This, of course, was characteristic of Mary Queen of Scots, who could not be persuaded to renounce Bothwell.

Throckmorton, in a letter to Elizabeth, July 1564, says :

" The queen will not by any means be induced to lend her authority to prosecute the murder, nor will not consent by any persuasion to abandon the lord Bothwell for her husband, but avoweth constantly that she will live and die with him and sayeth that if it were put to her choice to relinquish her crown and kingdom for the lord Bothwell she would leave her kingdom and dignity to live as a simple damoiselle with him and that she will never consent that he shall fare worse or have more harm than herself."

So Throckmorton says again to Elizabeth :

" She will by no means yield to abandon Bothwell for her husband, nor relinquish him ; which matter will do her most harm of all and hardneth these lords to great severity against her."

So the Lords of Scotland communicate to Sir Nicholas Throckmorton, July 1567 :

" We began to deal with her majesty, and to persuade her that, for her own honour, the safety of her son, the discharging of her conscience . . . she would be content to separate herself from that wicked man, to whom she was never lawfully joined, and with whom she could not remain without a manifest loss of honour . . . but all in vain."

Throckmorton himself repeatedly states to Elizabeth that the Lords were willing to be lenient to Mary personally.

" I have also persuaded herself to renounce Bothwell for her husband and to be contented to suffer a divorce to pass between them ; she hath sent me word that she will in no wise consent to it but will rather die."

It is impossible not to see the likeness between this

and Hamlet's expostulation with the queen,[1] when he
reproaches her with the dishonour she has brought upon
herself, appeals to her conscience, and finally implores
her to leave his uncle :

> " Good-night : but go not to mine uncle's bed ;
> . . . Refrain to-night,
> And that shall lend a kind of easiness
> To the next abstinence ; the next more easy."

Once again there is no parallel whatever in the original
prose source.

One more curious detail may be added.

Claudius, in *Hamlet*, is specially associated with three
courtiers called respectively, Osric,[2] Rosencrantz, and
Guildenstern,[3] and among the people who received the
captured Bothwell in Denmark was a certain " Eric
Rosencrantz." [4]

I have already pointed out that there was a Guildenstern
at the court of Scotland.

Before leaving, finally, the subject of the Darnley
murder, it is important to remember that James I. and
Bothwell were, from the outset, pitted against each other
by their respective supporters. The prince, though only
an infant, was legally represented as demanding vengeance
for his murdered father, and Bothwell was very generally
supposed to have designs upon his life.

" Bothwell after his marriage to the queen," says Sir
James Melville, " was very earnest to get the Prince in his
hands but my Lord of Mar would not deliver him, praying
me to help to save the Prince out of their hands who had

---

[1] Act III., iv.　　　　[2] Act V., ii.　　　　[3] Act IV., ii.
[4] *Les Affeires du Conte de Bodwel* (Bannatyne Club).

slain his father and had made his vaunt already among his familiars that, if he could get him once in his hands, he should warrant him from revenging of his father's death."

Similarly the proclamation issued 1567 by the Confederate Lords said that Bothwell had murdered the king, had entrapped the queen into an "unhonest marriage," and had made preparations "to commit the like murther upon the son as was upon the father."

At the battle of Carberry Hill the Confederate Lords had, as their standard, their favourite picture of the murdered man and of the infant prince kneeling by the side of the corpse, and demanding vengeance.

CHAPTER III

JAMES I. AND HAMLET

AND now I will turn to what has always been acknowledged as the crucial problem of the drama: the character of the hero himself, his melancholy and irresolution. The main problem of *Hamlet* always has been to determine why Hamlet does *not* act. He knows what he ought to do ; he himself realises it fully. Why does he not complete his task ? Does he hesitate, as Goethe thinks, because of a fineness of nature too great for the coarseness of the task which is thrust upon him ? Does he hesitate, as he himself accuses himself, out of mere slothfulness ? Does he hesitate, as Coleridge suggests, because in him the powers of thought have so far outweighed the powers of action that he cannot act ? Does he hesitate because incipient insanity is sapping his intellect ? All these points of view have been advanced, have been discussed at length in volume after volume. Mr Bradley, in his *Shakespearean Tragedy*, has reviewed many of them with admirable cogency, and in *The Problem of Hamlet* Mr J. M. Robertson has shown that in his opinion the inconsistencies in the character of Hamlet cannot be really reconciled, which he explains by the fact that Shakespeare is working over material set for him by an early play.

A study of Furness's " Variorum Edition " of *Hamlet* will

show how numerous these explanations are, and how very greatly they vary.

My own suggestion would be that *Hamlet* was probably a great deal simpler for Shakespeare's audience to understand than it is for us ; they carried in all likelihood a commentary in their own minds which enabled them to comprehend it more easily than we can. Tolstoy has, in fact, accused Shakespeare of *not* being a great artist,[1] precisely because *Hamlet* is so difficult to understand ; now as Shakespeare was not only a great artist, but, also, as we know him to have been, a popular dramatist of intense appeal, the difficulty is probably one which exists mainly for later commentators and did not exist to the same extent for the original audience.

My own explanation of the central theme of the play would be that Shakespeare was stating with unexampled force and cogency an historical problem which neither he nor any member of his audience possessed at that time the data for quite adequately solving. It is my purpose to show, however, that the problem was essentially historical and political. Let us first observe clearly one point ; there is not a hint or shadow of the main problem in the prose source.

In Saxo Grammaticus and the *Hystorie of Hamblet* alike the task before the hero is perfectly simple and the difficulties are all obvious and material. The hero desires to avenge his father's murder and he desires to gain for himself the crown which his uncle has usurped ; he pursues these aims with relentless determination and undeviating skill ; but, since he is isolated among enemies,

[1] *What is Art ?*

he shams madness as a means of putting these enemies off the scent, and his madness takes the most grotesque and ridiculous form.

Saxo says :

" Every day he remained in his house utterly listless and unclean, flinging himself on the ground and bespattering his person with foul and filthy dirt. His discoloured face and visage smutched with slime denoted foolish and grotesque madness.

" . . . He used at times to sit by the fire and rake the embers with his hands."

The *Hystorie of Hamblet* is still more extravagant :

" hee rent and tore his clothes, wallowing and lying in the dust and mire, his face all filthy and blacke, running through the streets like a man distraught, not speaking one word but such as seemed to proceed from madness and mere frenzy."

We can see at once the enormous difference between this coarse and crude representation and the subtlety of Hamlet.

Now let us compare the character of Hamlet carefully with what was, at that time, known of James I.

There is, as already pointed out, the fact of education at a university specially associated with Protestant theology ; James himself was, of course, all his life famous as a Protestant theologian ; he took part in theological discussions, he presided at theological discussions, and he showed marked ability in argument.

Hamlet is the most philosophic and meditative of all Shakespeare's characters, and he shows a curious love of the darker side of nature.

Now James was the pupil of a distinguished scholar —Buchanan; he took all his life a great interest in philosophy, and he was, as his books show, especially fond of studying the darker side of nature.

James was, in his early life at least, much isolated; there was hardly anyone whom he really trusted except possibly Erskine of Mar, in whom he had immense confidence, and with whom he had been educated. So Shakespeare represents Hamlet as being lonely and isolated; but as having one friend in whom he reposes perfect confidence and absolute trust—that one friend being his fellow-student—Horatio.

This second Earl of Mar was the son of the first Earl who had rescued James in his infancy from the hands of Bothwell as recounted above; this second Earl having been James' own fellow-student, it was to him that he entrusted the education of Prince Henry. We may also observe that Mar was in England at the time *Hamlet* was written; he had been sent by James to confer with Essex; when he arrived, however, he found that Essex had already been executed, and he chose his own line of action, his aim being to get his master's right to the succession established; Elizabeth is said to have given him the promise he required.

On March 25th, Tobie Matthew writes to Dudley Carleton :

" The Earl of Mar is here, as ambassador out of Scotland, to congratulate the queen's deliverance, to desire that his master may be declared successor, and to act, as is conjectured, some greater business which is likely enough, for he is a man of extraordinary courage and place."

Now, when we remember that Mar was actually in England at the time *Hamlet* was composed, and that Shakespeare had every reason for furthering his mission, it does look as if he might have given hints for Horatio—the trusted friend and fellow-student.

The most peculiar trait in Hamlet's character is his vacillation. He knows how he ought to act, yet he hesitates whenever action is necessary; on the other hand, he has plenty of nerve in important crises; when a crisis arrives he can act, and often does act, with quite exceptional strength and vigour.

Professor Bradley analyses at some length this extraordinary contradiction; he does not find Hamlet essentially the meditative, irresolute person whom Coleridge and Schlegel believe him to be; he finds that he has a capacity for strong and vigorous action which is, however, lamed by his melancholy :

" This state accounts for Hamlet's energy as well as for his lassitude, these quick decided actions of his being the outcome of a nature normally far from passive, now suddenly stimulated and producing healthy impulses which work themselves out before they have time to subside."

Examples of this sudden vigorous action are, of course, Hamlet's behaviour in the Rosencrantz and Guildenstern affair, also his conduct at the end of the play, etc., etc.

Now, this curious baffling character, this hesitancy and delay combined with sudden vigour in emergencies, is just precisely the character of James I. as it appeared to his contemporaries.

Perhaps the best evidence on this point can be found in the correspondence of Elizabeth and James. We there find Elizabeth, in letter after letter, taking almost precisely this view of James' character ; she advises him to be stern and to punish where punishment is due ; it is not, she declares, that she herself loves bloodshed or revenge ; but it is a monarch's duty both to himself and to his kingdom that he should punish rebellious subjects. She warns James that the younger Bothwell (the nephew of his mother's husband), has repeatedly plotted against his life; he knows that Bothwell has so conspired ; he knows that his life is endangered.

Why does he not take adequate means to defend himself and his kingdom ? His delay is not so much mercy as slothfulness and sheer weakness of will. It is unkingly. He talks, but achieves nothing.

Let me quote some highly significant examples :

" If with my eyes I had not viewed these treasons I should be ashamed to write them you. And shall I tell you my thought herein ? I assure you, you are well worthy of such traitors, that, when you knew them and had them, you betrayed your own safety in favouring their lives. Good Lord ! who but yourself would have left such people to be able to do you wrong ? Give order with speed, that such scape not your correction." [1]

We may compare this with Hamlet's bitter self-reproaches : [2]

> " I . . .
> A dull and muddy-mettled rascal, peak,
> Like John-a-dreams, unpregnant of my cause,
> And can say nothing ; . . .

---

[1] Camden Society's Publications. Letter XXXIV. (spelling modernised).

[2] Act II., ii.

> it cannot be
> But I am pigeon-liver'd and lack gall
> To make oppression bitter."

Let us keep in mind all the time that there is not one word of this reproach or hesitation in Shakespeare's source. The hero of the saga story pits himself as directly as possible against the king ; he is delayed by external circumstances solely, never by his own fault ; indeed, the whole point of the tale lies in the courage and decision of the prince who pursues his plan with undeviating resolution in the midst of the most difficult circumstances, and we have no reason to assume any difference in the Hamlet of Kyd's play.

Again let us quote Elizabeth [1] :

" I hope you will not be careless of such practises as hath passed from any of yours without your commission, specially such attempts as might ruin your realm and danger you. If any respect whatever make you neglect so expedient a work, I am afraid your careless hide will work your unlooked danger."

Place this beside Hamlet [2] :

> " How all occasions do inform against me,
> And spur my dull revenge ! What is a man,
> If his chief good and market of his time
> Be but to sleep and feed ?   A beast, no more.
>   . . . Now, whether it be
> Bestial oblivion, or some craven scruple
> Of thinking too precisely on the event,—
> A thought which, quarter'd, hath one part wisdom
> And ever three parts coward, I do not know
> Why yet I live to say ! ' This thing's to do,'
> Sith I have cause and will and strength and means
> To do't."

---

[1] Letter XXXV.   [2] Act IV., iv.

Hamlet, in fact, is as candid with himself as Elizabeth is with James; the mental malady which they are analysing appears to be of exactly the same type. The main outlines of James' character, as shown by his actions, were, of course, known to every one who followed public affairs ; Shakespeare was certainly no less keen a student of character than Elizabeth and the analysis which would be possible to her would be equally possible to the poet.

Again we quote Elizabeth. The occasion of the next letter is described as follows by Mr Tytler :

" Attacking the palace of Holyrood at the head of his desperate followers Bothwell had nearly surprised and made prisoners both the king and his chancellor. . . . An alarm was given, the king took refuge in one of the turrets, the chancellor barricaded his room and bravely beat off his assailants ; whilst the citizens of Edinburgh, headed by their provost, rushed into the outer court of the palace, and, cutting their way through the outer ranks of the borderers, compelled Bothwell to precipitate flight."

Elizabeth's letter runs :

" My dear brother. Though the hearing of your most dangerous peril be that thing that I most reverently render my most lowly thanks to God that you, by his mighty hand, hath scaped yet hath it been no other hazard than such as both hath been foreseen and foretold. . . . I know not what to write, so little do I like to lose labour in vain ; for if I saw counsel avail or aught pursued in due time or season, I should think my time fortunately spent to make you reap the due fruit of ripe opportunity ; but I see you have no look to help your state nor to assure you from treason's leisure. You give too much respite to rid your harm or shorten other's haste. Well : I will pray for you that God will unseal your eyes that have too long been shut."

Here, again, we have a situation very closely parallel to the one in *Hamlet*, and all these letters are connected, be it noted, with the younger Bothwell.

The younger Bothwell had been practising against the life and liberty of James almost exactly as Claudius practised against the life of Hamlet ; but the most open practices, the most manifest insults, cannot sting James into action.   Elizabeth is filled with wonder and horror that a monarch can submit to such insults.

So Hamlet accuses himself of submission to insult : [1]

> " Am I a coward ?
> Who calls me villain ?   Breaks my pate across ?
> Plucks off my beard, and blows it in my face ?
> Tweaks me by the nose ? gives me the lie i' the throat,
> As deep as to the lungs ? who does me this ?
> Ha !
> 'Swounds I should take it."

After the conspiracy known as the "Spanish Blanks" Elizabeth writes to James :

> " If you do not rake it to the bottom, you will verify what many a wise man hath (viewing your proceedings) judged of your guiltiness of your own wrack. . . .
> " I have beheld of late, a strange dishonourable and dangerous pardon which, if it be true, you have not only neglected yourself but wronged me ! "

Another letter of vehement expostulation seems to belong to the year 1592 when James had been literally driven from place to place by the factious Bothwell [2] :

> " To redouble crimes so oft, I say, with your pardon, must to your charge, which never durst have been renewed if the

---

[1] Act II., ii.   [2] Letter XLIV.

first had received the condign reward ; for slacking of due correction engenders the bold minds for new crimes. . . . I hear of so uncouth a way taken by some of your conventions, yea agreed to by your selfe that I must wonder how you will be clerk to such lessons.

" . . . O Lord, what strange dreams hear I that would God they were so, for then at my waking I should find them fables. If you mean, therefore, to reign I exhort you to show yourself worthy of the place which never can be surely settled without a steady course held to make you loved and feared. I assure myself many have escaped your hands more for dread of your remissness than for love of the escaped ; so oft they see you cherishing some men for open crimes and so they mistrust more their revenge than your assurance. . . . And since it so likes your to demand my counsel, I find so many ways your state so unjoynted, that it needs a skilfuller bone-setter than I to joyne each part in its right place."

One may compare this with Hamlet's bitter cry [1] :

> " The time is out of joint : O cursed spite
> That ever I was born to set it right."

In exactly the same way as Elizabeth piles up the indignities James has suffered, so Hamlet piles up those he endures himself [2] :

> " How stand I then,
> That have a father kill'd, a mother stain'd,
> Excitements of my reason and my blood,
> And let all sleep ? while to my shame I see
> The imminent death of twenty thousand men,
> That, for a fantasy and trick of fame,
> Go to their graves like beds."

In another letter Elizabeth points out to him how his laxness has caused corruption in the whole state :

" A long-rooted malady, falling to many relapses, argues,

---

[1] Act I., v.   [2] Act IV., iv.

F

by reason that the body is so corrupt that it may never be sound. When great infections light on many it almost poisons the whole country." [1]

Compare this with Hamlet:

> "How weary, stale, flat and unprofitable
> Seem to me all the uses of this world!
> Fie on't! ah fie! 'tis an unweeded garden,
> That grows to seed; things rank and gross in nature
> Possess it merely." [2]

Again Elizabeth says:

"If the variableness of Scotch affairs had not inured me with too old a custom I should never leave wondering at such strange and uncouth actions; but I have so oft with careful eyes foreseen the evil-coming harms and . . . see them either not believed or not redressed that I grow weary of such fruitless labour. One while I receive a writ of oblivion and foregiveness, then a revocation, with new additions of later consideration; sometimes, some you call traitors with proclaim, and anon, there must be no proof allowed, though never so apparent, against them."

Here, again, we have the likeness to Hamlet. Hamlet has proof after proof of the king's guilt, yet always demands more and more and is never, apparently, satisfied.

"What thank may they give your mercy," Elizabeth continues, "when no crime is tried? . . . And for Bothwell, Jesus! Did ever any muse more than I, that you could so quietly put up so temerous, indigne, a fact, and yet by your hand receiving assurance that all was pardoned and finished, I refer me to my own letter what doom I gave thereof. And now to hear all revoked and either scanted or denied and the wheel to turn to as ill a spoke." [3]

---

[1] Letter XLVIII.   [2] Act I., ii.
[3] Quoted from Tytler, Answer LIII.

Yet again (1593), James pardons Bothwell, and Elizabeth replies in the height of impatience and anger :

"My Dear Brother—To see so much, I rue my sight, that views the evident spectacle of a seduced king, abusing council and wry-guided kingdom. . . .

"I doubt whether shame or sorrow have had the upper hand when I read your last lines to me. . . . Abuse not yourself so far. . . . Assure yourself no greater peril can ever befall you, nor any king else, than to take for payment evil accounts ; for they deride such and make their prey of your neglect. There is no prince alive, but if he show fear or yielding but he shall have tutors enough though he be out of minority. And when I remember what sore punishment these lewd traitors should have, then I read again, lest at first I mistook your mind ; but when the reviewing granted my lecture true, Lord ! what wonder grew in me, that you should correct them with benefits who deserve much severer correction. . . . Is it possible that you can swallow the taste of so bitter a drug more meet to purge you of them, than worthy of your kindly acceptance.

"I never heard a more deriding scorn."

Here, again, Elizabeth wonders at the disgraces and scorns to which James will submit just precisely as Hamlet wonders why he submits to such infamies and shames.

Does it not look as if the mental malady in the two were identical ? Elizabeth and Shakespeare were both people of genius and they were analysing one and the same case.

We may quote here an incident, no doubt among those alluded to by the queen, which seems to have an important bearing on *Hamlet* :

"On 21st July sentence of forfeiture was passed against him (Bothwell) by parliament, all his property being con-

fiscated, and his arms riven at the cross of Edinburgh. His
friends thereupon determined to make a special effort upon
his behalf.   The Duke of Lennox and other noblemen secretly
sympathised with him, on account of their jealousy of Maitland.
On the evening of the 24th, after assembling their retainers
in the neighbourhood of the palace, Bothwell in disguise was
introduced into the king's chamber during his temporary
absence. On returning, the king found Bothwell on his
knees, with his drawn sword laid before him crying with a
loud voice for pardon and mercy.

" The king called out ' Treason ' ; the citizens of Edinburgh
hurried in battle array into the inner court ; but the king,
pacified by the assurances of those in attendance on him,
commanded them to retire.   Bothwell persisted that he
did not come in ' any manner of hostility, but in plain
simplicity.'

" To remove the king's manifest terror he offered to depart
immediately and remain in banishment, or in any other part
of the country till his day of trial.

" The king permitted him to leave and an act of condonation
and remission was passed in his favour but . . . the king
remained ' in perpetual grief of mind,' affirming that he
was virtually the captive of Bothwell and the other noblemen
who had abetted him. . . .

" On 14th August, he signed an agreement binding himself
to pardon Bothwell and his adherents, and to restore them to
their estates and honours, the agreement to be ratified by a
parliament to be held in the following November ; but at a
convention held at Stirling on 8th September an attempt
was made to modify the bargain, it being set forth as a condition of Bothwell's restoration that he should remain beyond
seas during the king's pleasure.   Matters soon drifted into
the old unsatisfactory condition." [1]

Now, here we surely have a very close approximation
to one of the most curious scenes in *Hamlet*. James has
suffered all kinds of outrages and indignities from the

[1] *Dict. Nat. Biog.*

younger Bothwell who has plotted against his life ; at last
he has Bothwell on his knees before him, and apparently
at his mercy ; Bothwell implores pardon and James
hears the prayer and spares him ; but he does not and
cannot alter their real relations which, soon after, assume
the same unsatisfactory character.

So Hamlet finds Claudius upon his knees, at prayer
and defenceless ; he has Claudius at his mercy and could
destroy him ; he spares him for the time, making the
excuse that he does not want to send his soul to heaven ;
all the same he knows that Claudius plots against his
life, and that he is practically helpless in his toils ; in no
real sense are their relations altered.

In 1595 Bothwell's position became desperate :

" His association with the Catholic earls proved fatal.
The king demanded his excommunication by the kirk and
although Bothwell wrote to the clergy of Edinburgh offering
to receive their correction for whatever offence he had committed he was on 18th February excommunicated by the
presbytery of Edinburgh at the king's command."

It looks very much as if this incident had suggested
Hamlet's determination to spare Claudius until he had
achieved his religious ruin, until he finds him about some
act " that has no relish of salvation in't " ; this incident
has startled many of Shakespeare's commentators who
cannot believe that Hamlet is stating his motive correctly
because it would be " too horrible " ; but if Shakespeare is simply dramatising history, then all we can
say is that the parallel is remarkably complete. James
did find Bothwell on his knees and at his mercy ; he did
spare him, and he spared him until the time when

Bothwell, at the king's request, was excommunicated and his religious ruin achieved.

There is no trace of such an incident either in Saxo Grammaticus or in the *Hystorie of Hamblet*.

Bothwell, one may note, had very often professed friendship towards the king, and had declared it impossible to hate " where both benefits and blood compelled him to love." [1]

One may compare this with the bitter irony of Hamlet's :

" A little more than kin and less than kind."

Elizabeth, as we have seen from the letters already quoted, was continually pointing out to James that he did not do his duty by his kingdom; the younger Bothwell provided the most conspicuous example of this neglect, but there were many other instances. The final result is that James' realm goes from bad to worse.

" Weeds in the fields, if they be suffered, will quickly overgrow the corn, but subjects being dandled, will make their own reigns and forlet another reign." [2]

Compare this once again with Hamlet's cry :

" How weary, stale, flat and unprofitable
  Seem to me all the uses of this world !
  Fie on't : ah fie ! 'tis an unweeded garden,
  Grown to seed ; things rank and gross in nature
  Possess it merely."

The resemblances between the situation dramatised in *Hamlet* and the situation revealed in the letters of Elizabeth are so close that we might almost believe that Shakespeare had been leaning over the queen's shoulder while she wrote.

[1] *Dict. Nat. Biog.*   [2] Letter LVII.

Surely the most obvious explanation of such coincidences is that they were analysing the same curious mentality.

In this connection I may refer to Mr Bradley, who points out that there is undoubtedly a large element of lethargy in the character of Hamlet :

" We are bound to consider the evidence which the text supplies of this, though it is usual to ignore it. When Hamlet mentions, as one possible cause of his inaction, his ' thinking too precisely on the event,' he mentions another ' bestial oblivion,' and the thing against which he inveighs in the greater part of that soliloquy (IV., iv.) is not the excess and misuse of reason (which for him here and always is godlike) ; but his *bestial* oblivion or *dullness*, this letting all sleep, this allowing of heaven-sent reason to ' fust unused.'

> ' What is a man,
> If his chief good and market of his time,
> Be but to sleep and feed ? a beast, no more.'

" So, in the soliloquy (II., ii.) he accuses himself of being ' a dull and muddy-mettled rascal ' who ' peaks like John-a-dreams unpregnant of his cause,' dully indifferent to his cause. So, when the Ghost appears to him the second time, he accuses himself of being tardy and lapsed in *time* ; and the Ghost speaks of his *purpose* as being almost *blunted* and bids him not to forget." [1]

On the ordinary supposition that *Hamlet* is simply a psychological problem which happened to interest Shakespeare at the time, it has always been somewhat difficult to comprehend how the play could appeal to great popular audiences in the way it undoubtedly did, for it was one of the most frequently acted of all Shakespeare's tragedies.

[1] *Shakespearean Tragedy.*

Revenge tragedies were common, but they were, as a rule, sufficiently simple in their appeal. Now Mr Robertson divines, in Kyd's original *Hamlet*, almost exactly such a tragedy where the stress was laid, as it is in Saxo and in the *Hystorie of Hamblet*, mainly upon the motive of revenge.

But the problem dramatised in *Hamlet* is one of singular subtlety and complexity; it is the problem of a man who sees what he ought to do, and yet cannot do it; who permits people to heap upon him outrage after outrage, insult upon insult, and yet does not punish even when he has the offender in his power; it is the problem of one who is ready to give the benefit of every doubt, who cannot believe even in reiterated evidences of crime and who, even when he is convinced, still goes on pardoning.

Is the incapacity for action due to the fineness of a too refined nature in its conflict with a coarse world? Is it mere sloth and cowardice and a want of princely, nay, of human dignity? Certainly Hamlet does not spare himself.

Whatever the solution of the problem may be, there is no doubt that the problem itself is the central interest of Shakespeare's play, and that there is not a trace of it in the original story. In the Amleth Saga the hero has to employ devious methods to attain his purpose; but in the purpose itself he never falters or wavers, and we have no reason to imagine that the hero of Kyd's play differed greatly. To make the incapacity for action the very centre of a tragedy was a startling innovation, and a most curious and subtle problem to bring before a popular audience. But, if the problem were really historical, if the problem concerned the character of the man whose succession to the crown was just then the chief question of practical politics, if the problem concerned the character of their own future monarch upon whom all the destiny of England, the destiny of each member of the audience, essentially depended, we can understand at once why Shakespeare selected a subject so unusual, and why it so greatly fascinated both his audience and himself.

At any rate, one thing is certain. Shakespeare's central problem does not, so far as we know, exist in *any* of his so-called sources ; it does exist in the history —unmistakeable, definite and clear; moreover, it was the precise historical problem which, at the exact moment *Hamlet* was written, was likely to interest Shakespeare's audience most.

It may, of course, be only coincidence ; but this seems to me very improbable ; a great dramatist is not a person working in a void, independent of time and space ; every great dramatist has to deal with two materials : one is the stuff or substance of his own dramatic genius, the other is the mentality of his audience.

It is and must be a main part of dramatic genius to utilise the susceptibilities and interests of the audience in the fullest way possible.

Now, suppose that Shakespeare really desires to do this. His audience, just at that moment, are probably more interested in the question of the Scottish succession and the Essex conspiracy than in anything else upon earth. Suppose he wishes to avail himself of this interest and to dramatise Scottish history and the character of James.

How will he set about it ?

From the point of view of drama history is too diffuse ; its interest is distracted and dissipated.

Thus the situation of James whose father has been murdered, and whose mother has married his father's murderer, this situation is, in itself, an intensely interesting one, the more so as the prince himself is claimed as " the avenger of his father " ; dramatically considered the situation has, however, one serious flaw—the flaw that the prince is an infant at the time, and cannot possibly pursue in person this "vengeance."

Again, the whole of the relations between James and the younger Bothwell are singularly interesting as an illustration of the character of James—the doubts, the hesitancy, the reluctance to punish, the demanding ever fresh and fresh proofs, which proofs never satisfy, the refusal to be roused even by insults, even by manifest plots against his own life, all this is exceedingly interesting ; but it is really quite a different story from the story of his father's murder, and to put them both into a drama would be, quite inevitably, to diffuse and break the dramatic interest.

It could not make a good play.   An excellent drama can, however, be made by combining in one the parts played by the two Bothwells.   There is nothing difficult in such a conception : the two belonged to the same family,[1] they were uncle and nephew, they held the

---

[1] The younger Bothwell on the mother's side ; on the father's he was a Stuart.

same title ; they were not very dissimilar in character ;
even modern Scottish historians have remarked that the
younger Bothwell seemed like a reincarnation of the elder.

The device of putting the two in one is quite simple
and obvious, and makes excellent drama : the crimes
committed by Claudius are the crimes of the *elder* Bothwell
which are far more striking and dramatic than the crimes
of the younger Bothwell ; but the relation of Hamlet to
Claudius is the relation of James to the *younger* Bothwell.
Why not ?   James was neglecting his duty to his
kingdom just as thoroughly as Hamlet was neglecting
his duty to his father, only the latter happens to be the
thing which can, most effectively, be put upon the stage.

Thus, instead of two stories with their interests diffused,
we have one story with its interest enormously concentrated.   And there is this further advantage, that
whereas no censorship would permit Shakespeare to
dramatise Scottish history as it really occurred, the
censorship could not prevent him from dramatising
history, if he altered it to some extent, and called it
Hamlet.

This, it seems to me, is the essential part of the play,
and this is the real reason why Shakespeare borrows a
name and a situation and practically nothing else from
the Amleth Saga.

A similar method of construction is, we may point
out, suggested by Shakespeare himself and in *Hamlet*
also ; it is Hamlet's own method of dealing with the
Gonzago story ; he selects a tale which resembles very
closely indeed the actual details of his father's murder,
he alters it to make it more like, and then, when the

king is filled with horror and anger, Hamlet insists that
" the story is extant and writ in choice Italian."

When we remember that this was exactly the method
which Shakespeare and his company were in disgrace
for employing in the case of *Richard II.*, we must surely
admit that our evidence is cumulative.

There are many other resemblances to the character
of James which may also be developed.

Thus, as Professor Bradley has pointed out, the
character of Hamlet, notwithstanding its curious
hesitancy and indecision, shows a singular power of
acting in sudden crises with vigour and strength ; it is
as of a sudden emergency let loose a different strain in
his nature ; thus, when he is on the voyage to England,
he guesses the plan of the king against him, and substitutes for his own name as the name of the person to
be executed those of his two companions.

The type of morality involved in this particular pro-
ceeding has seriously shocked some critics ; but here
we need only refer to it as proving Hamlet's capacity
for swift action in emergency ; it is one of the few things
that Shakespeare takes directly from the saga, and it
has something about it of peculiar crudity but it serves
to show that Shakespeare's full portrait of Hamlet included this power of swift action in emergency.

Similar power of swift and decisive action is, of course,
revealed in the final scene when Hamlet kills the king ;
after all the seemingly endless delays he rushes to the
point in a moment : " Then venom, do thy work," and
the work is done.

Now this peculiar contradiction, as we have seen,

was characteristic also of James, and was one of the things that most astonished his contemporaries.

Burton says :

" He was a very timid and irresolute man, and yet on more than one occasion he behaved with an amount of nerve and courage which the greatest of heroes could not have excelled. . . . People on the other side of the North Sea speak of his journey to bring home his wife as a thing which he surely would not have attempted had he known the perils of the coast of Norway in winter. Whether he knew what he incurred or not on that occasion, we have seen his conduct on another [1] when the peril was not of his own seeking. He held his own in the hand-to-hand struggle with young Ruthven. He reminded the young man of the presence he was in and the propriety of removing his hat. He corrected the mysterious man in armour when he was opening the wrong window. . . .

Finally the struggle had taught him that his assailant wore secret armour, so he told Ramsay to strike below it. It is known that men of a nervous temperament will, when at bay and desperate, become unconscious of their position, and act from a sort of mechanical influence, as if there were no danger near them. Are we so to account for these wonderful instances of presence of mind ? "

Here, again, we have a historical trait exactly similar to a trait noticeable in Hamlet.

Another curious trait in James's character was his indifference to dress. His mother had never been careless in this matter ; if not a lover of splendour in the same sense as Elizabeth, she had always been decorous and dignified and, on appropriate occasions, magnificent.

James was singularly careless and unkinglike, to such

[1] The Gowry Conspiracy.

an extent that he excited the derision of English visitors, and was jeered at for indecorum.

Sir Anthony Weldon says :

" In his diet, apparel and journeys he was very constant. In his apparel so constant as by his goodwill he would never change his clothes till almost worn out to rags . . . his fashion never ; inasmuch as one bringing to him a hat of a Spanish block, he cast it from him, swearing he neither loved them nor their fashions.   Another time, bringing him roses on his shoes, he asked them if they would make him a ruff-footed dove—one yard of sixpenny ribbon served that turn."

Here, again, it is impossible not to see the likeness to Hamlet : Hamlet's indifference to dress and his scorn for the courtiers to whom it means so much.

Ophelia speaks of him as wearing disordered apparel [1] :

" Lord Hamlet with his doublet all unbraced ;
No hat upon his head ; his stockings foul'd
Ungarter'd and down-gyved to his ancle ";

and Hamlet shows the utmost contempt for Osric " the water-fly," and for Rosencrantz and Guildenstern.

Other portions of Sir Anthony Weldon's description may also be quoted :

" He was very witty, and has as many ready, witty jests as any man living at which he would not smile himselfe, but deliver them in a grave and serious manner. . . .
" He would make a great deal too bold with God in his passion both in cursing and swearing and one strain higher verging on blasphemy ; but would in his better temper say : ' He hoped God would not impute them as sins and lay them to his charge, seeing they proceeded from passion.' "
" He was infinitely inclined to peace."
" His chosen motto was : ' Beati pacifici.' "

---

[1] Act II., i.

Here, again, we have traits which closely resemble those of Hamlet. Hamlet's wit and his ready jests are shown in many scenes. At the same time he does deliver his jests in a grave and serious manner ; particularly in his relations to Polonius and to Osric and Guildenstern he is full of irony.

We have several examples of his cursing with regard to the king ; he accuses himself,[1] of cursing like a whore or a scullion :

> " Must, like a whore, unpack my heart with words,
> And fall a-cursing, like a very drab,
> A scullion ! "

As examples of James' witty sayings Weldon quotes : " I wonder not so much that women paint themselves, as that when they are painted, men can love them."

We may compare Hamlet [2] : " God has given you one face and you make yourselves another."

Again, James was a student ; he was particularly fond, as we have seen, of discoursing on theology and philosophy ; he was also in the habit of taking tablets wherever he went to make notes ; his tablets were always on hand, and this was a marked peculiarity of his. Hamlet, also, has this peculiarity, and shows it in a most extraordinary manner ; he even carries his tablets with him in his interview with the ghost, and notes down the fact that

> " A man may smile and smile and be a villain " ;

it is surely the most extraordinary example recorded of the use of tablets and serves to show, at the least,

---

[1] Act II., ii.   [2] Act III., i.

that Hamlet must have been particularly addicted to their employment.   In fact, it is difficult to see any motive for such a bizarre example except to show a personal trait.

Hamlet is described by the queen as being " fat and scant of breath." James also was corpulent.   " He was of middle stature," says Sir Anthony Weldon, " more corpulent through his clothes than in reality, his body yet fat enough."

Hamlet is described as being thirty years of age,[1] for the sexton came to his office when young Hamlet was born and says : " I have been sexton here, man and boy, for thirty years."

James was actually about thirty-three when *Hamlet* was produced ; it was the custom, however, to state age in round numbers, and we occasionally find James mentioned as being thirty years of age when he came to the throne.[2]   This is almost the only case in Shakespeare where a definite age is given to the hero, and it looks as if there were a reason for it.

Again we observe Hamlet's curious methods of circumventing people, of finding out their intentions by means of tricks ; this is revealed most plainly in the case of Polonius ; but - the same thing happens with Osric, with Rosencrantz, and with Guildenstern, also with the king.

This, again, was a trait characteristic of James :

" If he had not that extreme timidity with which he has often been charged, he certainly shrank from facing dangers ; and this shrinking was allied in early life with a habit of

---

[1] Act V., i.

[2] See, for instance, *Secret History of Four Last Monarchs*, pub. 1691

cautious fencing with questioners, without much regard for truth, which was the natural outcome of his position among hostile parties." [1]

So Sir Anthony Weldon says of him : " He was very crafty and cunning in petty things, as the circumventing any great man."

This, surely, exactly resembles the position of Hamlet. Hamlet fences with Polonius, with the king, with Osric, with Rosencrantz, and certainly without much regard to the truth ; at the same time, it is justified to the mind of the audience by the manifest peril in which he stands and by the fact that the people who surround him are inimical and hostile, intent on betraying him ; the audience cordially approves of his trick of outwitting his enemies by verbal subtleties. Hamlet's policy delivers him from many perils, and James also earned the reward of a similar skill.

" He was," says Burton, " the first monarch of his race since the Jameses began who was to be permitted to reach the natural duration of his days ; for though his grandfather was not slain, his end was hastened by violence. When we trace the genealogic line of his house, we find it inaugurated by the murder of his father and the ruin of his mother, ending on the scaffold. . . ."

Now the James whom Shakespeare's audience were contemplating as their future king was the very person involved in these tragedies ; he had survived until his thirties, after being threatened with the most serious perils from and, indeed, even before his birth ; he had survived mainly by the devotion of a few most faithful

[1] *Dict. Nat. Biog.*

servants like the Erskines, and, from an extremely early age, by his own gifts ; his arts might savour of deceit, but they surely were permissible when the extreme danger and peril of his situation was taken into account : " he was the only one of his race since the Jameses began who was permitted to reach the natural duration of his days."

Could any words be stronger ?   Do they not correspond with the situation of Hamlet who has only one devoted friend, and who is surrounded by every form alike of violence and of treachery ?

But, it may be asked, if the character of Hamlet shows all these resemblances to that of James I., is it to be taken simply as a portrait ?

It does not seem to me that Shakespeare's method is essentially one of portraiture and, as I shall attempt to show later, I find other elements in the character of Hamlet besides what he owes to James.   It seems to me that the more accurate way of stating the matter would be to say that Shakespeare takes the main conception of Hamlet and the situation of Hamlet, from James and the situation of James.

The central situation, the Orestes-like motive of the play, that the murderer of the father has married the mother, is the situation of James ; the central problem of the play—the problem of the vacillating will, of the man who knows he ought to act but cannot act, of the man who is aware that he ought to punish but cannot punish—this is the problem of James's character.   That hatred of bloodshed which distinguishes Hamlet also, throughout his life, distinguished James ; again we have a similar love of philosophic discussion with an interest in spirits and the night-side of nature ; we have the same love of disputation with everybody whom he meets, the same parrying of indiscreet questions and escaping from difficult situations by means of verbal fence, the same feigning of stupidity which goes so far that he is sometimes suspected of madness ; we have a similar misogyny, we have the same curious power of swift and sudden action in crises notwithstanding the vacillations, we have the same power of pithy and witty sayings ; we have a similar carelessness of dress and a similar dislike of perfumed courtiers ; we have even minor details such as the habit of swearing, the use of tablets, the thirty years of age, the being " fat and scant of breath."

The point I wish to insist on is always that of the Elizabethan audience, and I ask, "Could they fail to see resemblances which are, on the one hand, so deep, profound and vital and, on the other hand, so curiously detailed ? "

It seems to me that the play of *Hamlet* is largely an appeal to their interest in their future king : a use for dramatic purposes of his history, his situation, and the leading traits in his character.

A rather curious point may be noted here. Attention has often been called to the close connection which appears to exist between *Hamlet* and *Measure for Measure*. Now, the character of the Duke in *Measure for Measure* also shows marked resemblances to that of James I. ; but there are two facts to be carefully observed ; one is that the character of the Duke is altogether inferior to that of Hamlet, it is not nearly so noble or so attractive, and the other is that the character of the Duke is more like that of the historic James as we usually conceive the latter to have been. I have dwelt on this elsewhere.[1]

Now, if Shakespeare takes the central conception of both these characters from the historic James, as he apparently does, the problem at once arises as to why these characters are in themselves so different.

Now it appears to me that the answer to this is probably threefold. In the first place, Shakespeare, when he wrote *Hamlet* had not seen James I.; at that date the Scottish king had not crossed the Border; all that was known of him must have been eagerly canvassed; but the man himself had never set foot in England. Before Shakespeare wrote *Measure for Measure*, both he and his audience had made the acquaintance of James, and had possibly found him less attractive on a nearer view. In the second place, Shakespeare quite probably intended *Hamlet*, in part at least, as a pamphlet in favour of the Scottish succession; in such circumstances he would naturally do everything he could to invest the figure of the prince with glamour and with charm; hence we have a philosophic and melancholy prince, seen against a background of dark crimes, a prince whose peace-loving nature makes him abhor the duty of blood-shed laid upon him, an enigmatic figure wayward and strange yet full of fascination.

What are our prevailing feelings as we pursue the course of the play? One of them surely is that we should

[1] *Measure for Measure*. (Heath of Boston.)

like to take Hamlet away from his surroundings which are unworthy of him, away from the Denmark which does not merit him, and introduce him to a nobler sphere.

But is not this precisely and exactly the feeling which Shakespeare wished to create? It is, at any rate, plausible.

In the third place, and perhaps most important of all, I do not consider that Hamlet is solely a portrait of James I.; it seems to me to contain much of Essex as Essex was in the last year of his life. I shall hope to demonstrate this later, and to show how those portions of the character which are psychologically inconsistent with the rest may have had their origin in this way. Here I need only state that I do not think *Hamlet* is a *portrait* of anyone.

CHAPTER IV

"THE PLAY WITHIN THE PLAY" AND HAMLET'S VOYAGE TO ENGLAND

I WILL pass on to a consideration of what seem like further historical resemblances in the drama.

After the Darnley murder, popular excitement showed itself in continually representing the scene of the murder, and thrusting these representations before the eyes of the people mainly concerned. The Lords of the Council exhibited a banner showing the two dead men—Darnley and his servant—beneath a tree, the little prince kneeling beside their bodies praying for vengeance, and a broken branch.

Burton says:

"A portion of the natural excitement of the time appears oddly enough to have expended itself in painting. Several representations seem to have been made of the discovery of the bodies, with more or less allegorical machinery; and several other pictures made their appearance which, either through an allegory or an attempt to represent facts, gave shape to the feelings of their producers. Caricatures they could not be called, for they had a deadly earnest about them . . . they were deemed as signs of the times so important that some of them may now be found among the documents of the period. There is one in which an attempt is made to represent the whole scene of the murder . . . the shattered house, the Hotel of the Hamiltons beside it, the city gate and wall, the remnant of the old Kirk-of-the-Field, the bodies and the assembled crowd of citizens."

The banner used by the Lords of the Council was employed at Carberry Hill as a kind of sacred symbol ; it was shown to Mary after her captivity, and produced a dreadful impression upon her.

Lingard says :

" An hour did not elapse before Mary learned that she was a captive in the hands of unfeeling adversaries. At her entrance into the city she was met by a mob in the highest state of excitement : her ears were assailed with reproaches and imprecations ; and before her eyes was waved a banner, representing the body of her late husband, and the prince her son on his knees exclaiming, " Revenge my cause, O Lord." . . . During the two and twenty hours that she was confined in her solitary prison, the unhappy queen abandoned herself to the terrors which her situation inspired. From the street she was repeatedly seen at the window almost in a state of nudity ; and was often heard to call on the citizens conjuring them to aid and deliver their sovereign from the cruelty of traitors."

Here, again, we surely have a very close likeness to the "play within the play" motive of Hamlet. Hamlet desires to reconstruct the murder before the very eyes of the guilty king ; since the whole drama is a stage presentation also, how else could it be shown ? The idea is exactly and precisely the same as that of the Scottish banners and paintings ; that of constructing graphic representations of the murder and thrusting them before the eyes of the guilty parties. We may observe, also, that Hamlet's play is largely a dumb show.

Hamlet cries, "The play's the thing wherein I'll catch the conscience of the king," and the Scottish accusers exhibited the dreadful scene on the banner in precisely this way, and with this motive, to the persons whose guilt was suspected but of whose participation they were not assured, and the result was precisely the same betrayal of grief and horror and anguish.

Nothing like this play scene appears in either Saxo Grammaticus or in the *Hystorie of Hamblet*, though it may have done in Kyd's play; but, as I have already pointed out, anything anterior to the supposed date of that play (1587 or 1589) may have been used by him as readily as by Shakespeare, and the Scottish parallel certainly might have been employed. If Shakespeare really wished to dramatise history it is difficult to see how he could have arranged the dramatisation better or more effectively, the essence being the scenic representation which forces the guilty to betray themselves.

I do not think this is the only historical reference in the part of *Hamlet* which relates to the players; but the rest will have its due study later.

Another historic parallel to be found in *Hamlet* is his voyage to England. This, of course, occurs in the original saga, but Shakespeare has changed its conclusion. In Saxo, Hamlet is sent to England with a secret message to the king, desiring him to put Hamlet to death; Hamlet, however, suspects the deceit, alters the message, and substitutes one desiring the king of England to give his daughter in marriage to the noble youth; " Nor was he satisfied with removing from himself the sentence of death, and passing the peril on to others, but added an entreaty that the king of Britain would grant his daughter in marriage to a youth of great judgment whom he was sending them."

In the *Hystorie of Hamblet*, we have exactly the same situation. All takes effect as Hamlet has planned.

The King, having witnessed many extraordinary examples of Hamlet's wisdom, gives him his daughter and Hamlet returns to his own country, takes his revenge, and ultimately, of course, claims his British bride :

> " Then the king adored the wisdom of Amleth as though it were inspired and gave him his daughter to wife ; accepting his bare word as though it were a witness from the skies."

Now, in the saga, the real purport of this journey to England is to get Hamlet married to an English princess ; Shakespeare removes this motive altogether, for his Hamlet does not marry, nevertheless he retains the voyage. There is thus a very curious effect produced.

Hamlet, who knows the designs the king has against his life, who knows that he ought to pursue his task of vengeance and punishment, nevertheless allows himself to be hurried out of the kingdom on a voyage which he must have been aware was excessively dangerous, from which he might never have returned. As more than one critic has pointed out this is most unfair to his unfortunate country ; he leaves it in the power of a villain while he allows himself to go, without any real necessity, on a most perilous expedition from which he is only saved by chance.

The effect is a curious mingling of hesitancy and rashness which is one of the difficulties of Hamlet's character and of the play. The whole adventure is without the strong, obvious and clear motive given in the saga. Why is it retained ? The answer would seem to be " because there is a real historical parallel and because this historical parallel did genuinely supply an important element in the character Shakespeare was studying."

James had received the promise of Anne of Denmark as his bride; the marriage by proxy was solemnised in August 1589. A brilliant little fleet was appointed for conveying the bride home to Scotland; but it was driven by storms into a port of Norway; James thereupon determined to set out himself to bring home his bride, and actually did so; the voyage at that time of the year was exceedingly dangerous, and the king's return was long delayed by storms.

In the meantime, the younger Bothwell had been left to his own devices in the kingdom.

Elizabeth blamed James as severely for his rashness in this episode as modern commentators have blamed Hamlet:

"I do believe that God hath of his goodness more than your hide, prospered to good end your untimely and, if I dare tell you the truth, evil-seasoned journey, yet I may no longer stay but let you know. . . . And now to talk to you freely as paper may utter conceit. Accept my hourly care for your broken country, too, too much infected with the malady of strange humours and to receive no medicine so well compounded as if the owner make the mixture appropriated to the quality of the sickness. Know you my dear brother, for certain, that those ulcers that were too much skinned with the ' doulceness " of your applications were but falsely shaded and were filled within with much venom as hath burst out since your departure with most lewd offers to another king to enter your land." [1]

Shakespeare has removed the clear, effective, and powerful motive which the voyage had in the saga. Yet

[1] Letter XXXIV.

he retains the incident. Why? It certainly looks as
if he had retained it as a temperamental trait because
it shows a power of vigorous action in emergency with,
at the same time, a certain rashness and weakness in the
very circumstances which enable the vigour to be shown.

It is interesting also to observe that the mysterious
letters have a historical parallel in the affair known as
the " Spanish blanks " which occurred shortly after
James' voyage.

Burton says :

" In the same year—1592—occurred the incident called
the " Spanish blanks " which disturbed the zealous Presby-
terian party to an extent not easily realised by looking at
the scanty materials by which it was produced. But in fact
it was the mystery excited by imperfect evidence that created
suspicion and terror. It was suspected that a man named
Kerr, who was leaving Scotland by the West coast, had
dangerous documents in his custody. The minister of Paisley,
hearing of this, gathered some sturdy parishioners who
seized and searched Kerr. They took from him eight papers
called " the blanks." Each had upon it the concluding
courtesies of a letter addressed to royalties. " De vostre
majestie tres humble et tres obesant servitor," and this was
followed by one or more signatures."

Otherwise these slips of paper had " no designation
on the back, nor declaration of the causes for which they
were sent, but blank and white paper on both sides except
the said subscriptions." They were signed by the
Catholic earls : Huntly, Errol, Angus, etc. The conclusion arrived at was that the blanks were intended to
be filled up by certain Jesuit emissaries and were, when
so filled, to form an invitation to the king of Spain to
send men to Scotland to assist in a Catholic rising.

James behaved in this affair according to his usual custom, and was particularly merciful to the offenders. Elizabeth, as her letters show, was greatly enraged, and once more demanded justice, but James punished no one.

Now here, again, one notices a marked difference between Shakespeare and his saga source.   In the saga there is no question whatever of Amleth being on good terms with the king after the treacherous embassy ; having discovered the truth, Amleth returns to Denmark and proceeds *at once* to his revenge.   He sets the banqueting hall on fire, burns most of the courtiers to death in their drunken sleep, and cuts off the head of the king in his own bedchamber.

Shakespeare's ever-forgiving Hamlet, however, once more places himself on amiable terms with Claudius and, for the last time, attempts friendship ; exactly in the same way James once more forgave the Catholic earls and Bothwell.

Once again we have a historic parallel.

CHAPTER V

POLONIUS, RIZZIO, AND BURLEIGH

OTHER portions of *Hamlet* which appear to contain historical reminiscences are the scenes connected with Polonius.

If the account of the murder, for instance, be carefully compared with the saga on the one hand, and with Scottish history on the other, it will be found, I think, that it shows hardly any resemblances to the one but very close resemblances to the other.

The saga reads :

" Feng was purposely to absent himself, pretending affairs of great import. Amleth should be closeted alone with his mother in her chamber ; but a man should first be commissioned to place himself in a concealed part of the room and listen heedfully to what they talked about. For, if the son had any wits at all, he would not hesitate to speak out in the hearing of his mother or fear to trust himself to the fidelity of her who bore him. The speaker . . . zealously professed himself as the agent of the eavesdropping. Feng rejoiced at the scheme and departed on pretence of a long journey. Now he who had given this counsel repaired privily to the room where Amleth was shut up with his mother, and lay down skulking in the straw. But Amleth had his antidote for the treachery. Afraid of being heard by some eavesdropper he at first resorted to his usual imbecile ways and crowed like a noisy cock, beating his arms together to mimic the flapping of wings. Then he mounted the straw and began to swing his body and jump again and again, wishing to try if aught lurked there in hiding. Feeling a lump beneath his feet he drove his sword into the spot and impaled him who lay hid. Then he dragged him from his concealment and slew him. Then, cutting his body into morsels, he seethed it in boiling water and flung it through the mouth of an open sewer for the swine to eat, bestrewing the stinking mire with his helpless limbs. . . .

"When Feng returned nowhere could he find the man who had suggested the treacherous espial; he searched for him long and carefully, but none said they had seen him anywhere. Amleth, among others, was asked in jest if he had come across any trace of him, and replied that the man had gone to the sewer but had fallen to its bottom and been stifled by the floods of filth, and that then he had been devoured by the swine that came up all about the place.[1]

The *Hystorie of Hamblet* gives substantially the same tale; it says that Hamlet cut the body into pieces, boiled it, and then cast it into an open vault or privy, so that it might serve as food for the pigs.

Now, here there is one point of resemblance with Shakespeare's *Hamlet*; that is the motive given to the eavesdropper who is to report Hamlet's confidences to his mother, but all the rest is entirely unlike.

What has Shakespeare's Hamlet in common with this grotesque clown who crows like a cock, and with this hideous barbarian who boils the body of his victim and then throws it through a sewer to the pigs?

Turn now to Scottish history and see what it says of the murder of Rizzio:

Signor David became the queen's inseparable companion in the council room and the cabinet. At all hours of the day he was to be found with her in her apartments. . . . He

---

[1] Saxo Grammaticus.

was often alone with her until midnight. He had the control
of all the business of the state. . . . Darnley went one night
between twelve and one to the queen's room. Finding the
door locked he knocked, but could get no answer . . . after
a long time the Queen drew the bolt . . . he entered and she
appeared to be alone but, on searching, he found Rizzio half-
dressed in a closet. . . . Darnley's word was not a good one,
but that was what he said. . . . Darnley desired the dramatic
revenge of killing Rizzio in the queen's presence. . . . The
conspirators ascended the winding stairs from Darnley's
room . . . Darnley entered . . . supper was on the table
. . . the queen asked Darnley if he had supped." [1]

So the scene proceeds ; Rizzio calls loudly for help,
but he is stabbed ; Darnley's dagger is left in the body
so that he may be clearly incriminated, the body itself
is dragged down a staircase and flung upon a chest. . . .
The queen lamented bitterly for him : " Poor David !
Good and faithful servant. May God have mercy on
your soul."

Afterwards, we may remember, Darnley was reconciled to the queen and showed or affected to show bitter
repentance for his share in the murder. The Lords
Politic sat for several days to consider the murder ;
but, since they feared to accuse anyone, nothing was
done.

Now, here, we surely have far closer resemblances
to the scene in *Hamlet* though, as in the other parallels,
the scene is dramatised by isolating and concentrating ;
two scenes are run into one, the scene where Darnley
alone discovered (or said he discovered) Rizzio, and the
scene of the murder.

[1] Froude.

We have the discovery by the hero alone, we have the stabbing with the hero's weapon in the dead man's body. We have the queen's bitter lament for the " good old man " [1] and for the " rash and bloody deed." Hamlet disposes of the body " by a staircase," and the staircase played a principal part in the Rizzio murder.

We may also observe that Hamlet's gruesome remark about Polonius being " at supper, not where he eats but where he is eaten," [2] seems like a macabre reference to the Rizzio murder where the victim also was found " at supper "; the same may be said of the remark that " a certain convocation of politic worms are e'en at him," which, again, looks like a macabre reference to the wearisome and futile sittings of the " Lords Politic " in considering the murder. Any of these references might be accidental if it stood alone; it is, as always, the *combination* which is the convincing thing.

We may observe that the intimacy of Polonius with the queen is really close; he is not, like the eavesdropper in the saga, a person with whom she has no intimate concern; he is a genuinely trusted councillor.

It may be said that the Rizzio murder belongs to Darnley and not to James I., but it had a close and vital connection with the group of historic events, and was in itself, a thing which probably determined the choice, magnificent dramatic material.

We may also observe that the whole scene is, as it were, set apart in the play and stands detached from the main action. There is, again, the statement that Hamlet

[1] Act IV., i.   [2] Act IV., iii.

repents his deed, for, according to the queen " he weeps for what is done," and she, at any rate, desires to shield and protect him. All this is foreign to the saga, but does occur in the history. Darnley professed penitence and the queen did protect him. I may also point out that the other reference to the Rizzio murder occurred in the first scene where the ghost appeared to Hamlet, and in this scene with the queen the ghost appears again. There is, apparently, a logical and dramatic connection between the two.

Moberley has a note on the lines :

> " Indeed this councillor
> Is now most still, most secret and most grave
> Who was in life a foolish prating knave."

He observes that they are almost exactly the same words used by the porter at Holyrood, when Rizzio's body was placed on a chest near his lodge.

But we do not, I think, dispose of the historical resemblances in the character of Polonius by saying that his death resembles that of Rizzio's. It has more than once been pointed out that he shows a likeness to Burleigh, and this, also, appears to be true. We may observe that Burleigh died in the year 1598, shortly before *Hamlet* was produced ; he had died at the advanced age of seventy-eight, and was thought by many to have been in his dotage ; even Elizabeth in her wrath occasionally accused him of dotage.[1]

Burleigh had been the bitter enemy of Shakespeare's

[1] Martin Hume, *Burleigh*.

H

patrons—Essex and Southampton, and it was generally believed that the Cecils between them had lured Essex to his ruin. The popular mind also ascribed to Burleigh enmity against the Scottish succession.

Now, if Burleigh were the bitter enemy of Shakespeare's friends, if he were very generally unpopular and mistrusted, if he were believed to be an enemy to the Scottish succession, Shakespeare might very naturally represent him as another of the main enemies of his philosophic prince, and that is what he appears to have done, for the resemblances between Burleigh and Polonius seem too great to be ascribed to any form of accident.

In the first place we may note that the original form of the name was Corambis and not Polonius, and that Corambis does suggest Cecil and Burleigh.

Polonius, throughout the play, stands isolated as the one person who does really enjoy the royal confidence; he is an old man, and no other councillor of equal rank anywhere appears. This corresponds almost precisely with the position held by Burleigh; he had, for the greater part of his reign, been among Elizabeth's chief councillors, and the death of Walsingham and others left him isolated in her service, surviving almost all the men of his own generation.

Cecil was a man of learning, and Polonius obviously desires to be esteemed as such. Cecil had been closely associated with some of the chief classical scholars of the day, Cheke for example, and Polonius makes a boast of his classical learning:[1] " Seneca cannot be too heavy, nor Plautus too light."

[1] Act II., ii.

Cecil, in his youth, had played a prominent part in Cambridge, and was proud to remain connected with the university, and Polonius also alludes to his life in the university and his taking part in the university plays.[1] " I did enact Julius Cæsar ; I was killed i' the Capitol ; Brutus killed me."

We may also remember, in this connection, that when William Cecil died, he was still Chancellor of the University of Cambridge ; there can be no doubt both from Hamlet's question, and from his reply, that Polonius liked to associate himself with the university as Cecil did.

Cecil had one romance, and one romance only, in his life, that was when he married a penniless bride—Mary Cheke, the sister of the great Greek scholar ; the marriage was vehemently opposed by his family, but Cecil espoused her in secret.

Now, according to his own account, Polonius also had experienced a romantic love-affair in his youth : '' truly in my youth I suffered much extremity for love, very near this." [2]

This particular speech has nearly always been considered as a pure absurdity ; but it would be even more ironically amusing if the audience believed it literally true.

Again, Burleigh's eldest son—Thomas Cecil—was a youth of very wayward life ; his licentiousness and irregularity occasioned his father great distress and, during his residence in Paris, his father wrote letters to him full of wise maxims for his guidance ; he also instructed friends to watch over him, and bring him

[1] Act III., ii.   [2] Act II., ii.

reports of his son's behaviour. So Polonius has a son
—Laertes—whom he suspects of irregular life ; Polonius
provides that his son, when he goes to Paris, shall be
carefully watched, and that reports on his behaviour
shall be prepared by Reynaldo.

I will place side by side the parallels that seem to
me most pertinent, pointing out first that there is no
resemblance *whatever* in the saga source.

" Amidst his manifold public anxieties Cecil had to bear
his share of private trouble. . . . Thomas, his only son by
his first marriage with Mary Cheke was now (1561) a young
man of twenty, and in order that he might receive the polish
fitting to the heir of a great personage, his father consulted
Sir Nicholas Throgmorton, the Ambassador in Paris, in the
Spring of 1561, with the idea of sending him thither. A
subsequent recommendation of Thomas Windebank, the
young man's governor, to the effect that it would be well to
accept Throgmorton's offer, although Sir William Cecil was
loath to trespass on his friend's hospitality, " in order that the
youth might learn, not only at table but otherwise, according
to his estate," leads us to the conclusion that Thomas Cecil
had not hitherto been an apt scholar . . . from the first it
was seen that the father was misgiving and anxious. Cecil
was a reserved man, full of public affairs ; but this correspondence proves that he was also a man of deep family
affections, and above all, that he regarded with horror the
idea that any scandal should attach to his honoured name.
In his first letter to his son he strikes the note of distrust. . . .
" He wishes him God's blessing, but how he inclines himself
to deserve it he knows not." None of his son's three letters,
he explains, makes any mention of the expense he is incurring.
. . . To Windebank the father is more outspoken. How
are they spending their time, he asks, and heartily prays that
Thomas may serve God with fear and reverence. But
Thomas seems to have done nothing of the sort ; for, in
nearly every letter, Windebank urges Sir William to repeat

his injunctions about prayer to his son. . . . But the scape-grace paid little heed. . . . Rumour of his ill-behaviour reached Sir William, not at first from Windebank. In March 1562 an angry and indignant letter went from Cecil to his son, reproaching him for his bad conduct. There was no amendment he said, and all who came to Paris gave him the character of " a dissolute, slothful, negligent and careless young man and the letter is signed ' your father of an un-worthy son.' "

A week later Cecil writes : " Windebank, I am here used to pains and troubles, but none creep so near my heart as does this of my lewd son. . . . Good Windebank, consult my dear friend Sir Nicholas Throgmorton, to whom I have referred the whole. . . . If ye shall come with him (*i.e.* Thomas) to cover the shame, let it appear to be by reason of the troubles there." [1]

We may compare this with *Hamlet* [2]:

POL. Give him this money and these notes, Reynaldo.
REY. I will, my lord.
POL. You shall do marvellous wisely, good Reynaldo,
Before you visit him, to make inquire
Of his behaviour.
REY. My lord, I did intend it.
POL. Marry, well said ; very well said.   Look you, sir,
Inquire me first what Danskers are in Paris ;
And how, and who, what means, and where they keep,
                              . . . and finding
By this encompassment and drift of question
That they do know my son, come you more nearer,
Than your particular demands will touch it :
                              . . . put on him
What forgeries you please ; marry, none so rank
As may dishonour him ; take heed of that ;

---

[1] Martin Hume, *Burleigh*.   [2] Act II., i.

But, sir, such wanton wild and usual slips
As are companions noted and most known
To youth and liberty.
REY. As gaming, my lord.
POL. Ay, or drinking, fencing, swearing, quarrelling,
Drabbing: you may go so far."

Now, surely we notice here an essentially similar situation to the one given in Burleigh's life ; the father an immaculate, all-wise councillor at home, the spendthrift son leading a licentious life in Paris, and anyone who knows the father encouraged to give reports on the son's behaviour which the father anticipates, with only too much justice, will almost certainly be evil reports.

Cecil wrote a number of maxims for the guidance of his son, and these maxims show a remarkable likeness to those given by Polonius to Laertes.

" If his own conduct was ruled," says Martin Hume, " as some of his actions were by the maxims which in middle age he had laid down for his favourite son, he must have been a marvel of prudence and wisdom. Like the usual recommendations of age to youth, many of these precepts simply inculcate moderation, religion, virtue and other obviously good qualities ; but here and there Cecil's own philosophy of life comes out, and some of the reasons for his success are exhibited. " Let thy hospitality be moderate . . . rather plentiful than sparing, for I never knew any man grow poor by keeping an orderly table. . . . Beware thou spendest not more than three of four parts of thy revenue, and not above a third part of that in thy house."

" Beware of being surety for thy best friends ; he that payeth another man's debts seeketh his own decay."

" Be sure to keep some great man thy friend, but trouble him not with trifles ; compliment him often with many, yet small gifts."

" Towards thy superiors be humble, yet generous ; with thine equals familiar yet respectful ; towards these inferiors show much humanity and some familiarity, as to bow the body, stretch forth the hand and to uncover the head."

" Trust not any man with thy life, credit or estate, for it is mere folly for a man to entrust himself to his friend."

We may compare with this Polonius [1] :

" Be thou familiar but by no means vulgar.
  Those friends thou hast and their adoption tried,
  Grapple them to thy soul with hoops of steel ;
  But do not dull thy psalm with entertainment.
  Of each new-hatch'd, unfledged comrade. Beware
  Of entrance to a quarrel; but being in,
  Bear't, that the opposed may beware of thee.
  Give every man thy ear, but few thy voice.

" Neither a borrower nor a lender be,
  For loan oft loses both itself and friend,
  And borrowing dulls the edge of husbandry."

Martin Hume sums up Burleigh's proverbs by saying :

" Such maxims as these evidently enshrine much of his own temper, and throughout his career he rarely seems to have violated them. His was a selfish and ungenerous gospel, but a prudent and circumspect one."

Exactly the same might be said of Shakespeare's Polonius. This particular fact, that the maxims of Polonius strongly resemble those of Burleigh—was pointed out by George Russell French in 1869.

Again, one observes the omnipresence of Polonius ; he manages everything, he interferes in everything, he

---

[1] Act I., iii.

keeps everything in his own hands. This was certainly true also of Cecil, who had a passion for detail :

" Everything seemed to pass through his hands. No matter was too small or too large to claim attention. His household biographer says of him that he worked incessantly, except at meal times when he unbent and chatted wittily to his friends, but never of business." [1]

Cecil had a peculiar method of drawing up documents touching matters of state : thus he would consider all the reasons for and against a particular action, stating its advantages and disadvantages in the most elaborate way and with meticulous care of detail. It is in just the same close and elaborate way that Polonius displays his ideas before the king. Everything is surveyed, not a detail omitted.[2]

" He repulsed—a short tale to make . . .
    Fell into a sadness, then into a fast,
    Thence to a watch, thence into a weakness,
    Thence to a lightness, and, by this declension,
    Into the madness wherein now he raves,
    And all we mourn for."

This is an admirable satire on the type of man who, like Cecil, prides himself on the logical, methodical development of detail.

Cecil was emphatically a man of peace ; in politics it was his great aim to keep out of war ; in private life he disliked the idea of a military career for his son Thomas, and he was a person with whom everybody found it very difficult to quarrel ; he kept the peace with Leicester, and with Essex in spite of infinite pro-

[1] Martin Hume.   [2] Act II., ii.

vocation ; Essex, especially, was given to taunting and
tormenting him ; but, when Cecil was unable to avoid
a quarrel in any other way, he was accustomed to
develop a timely fit of gout, and retire to his own house.

We see this same trait in Polonius who carefully
advises Laertes against quarrels : " Beware of entrance
to a quarrel," and who will put up with almost everything from Hamlet in order to avoid an overt dispute,
even, as Cecil did from Essex, with the most contemptuous
mocking.

Cecil employed spying and eavesdropping as political
weapons to a quite amazing extent :

"Spies and secret agents paid by him were in every court
and in every camp . . . the English Catholic nobles were
closely watched and for a month every line the Spanish
ambassador wrote was conveyed to Cecil by Borghese. Once,
early in May, the bishop's courier with important letters for
the Duchess of Parma, was stopped two miles beyond Graves-
end by pretended highwaymen who were really gentlemen
(the brothers Cobham) in Cecil's pay, and the man was
detained while the letters were sent to the Secretary to be
deciphered and copied." [1]

The *Dictionary of National Biography* states the matter
thus :

" His life began to be threatened ; assassins were bribed
to slay him and the queen : the murder of both or either, it
was taught, would be something more glorious than mere
justifiable homicide. Against the new doctrine and its
desperate disciples it seemed to Cecil that extraordinary
precautions were needed, and for the next twenty years he
kept a small army of spies and informers in his pay who were
his detective police, and he used it without scruple to get

---

[1] Martin Hume.

information when it was needed, to keep watch upon the sayings and doings of suspected characters at home and abroad. They were a vile band, and the employment of such instruments could not but bring some measure of dishonour upon their employer."

Intercepted letters and the employment of spies were, then, a quite conspicuous and notorious part of Cecil's statecraft, and they are certainly made especially characteristic of Shakespeare's Polonius. Polonius intercepts the letters from Hamlet to his daughter ; he appropriates Hamlet's most intimate correspondence, carries it to the king, and discusses it without a moment's shame or hesitation : he and the king play the eavesdropper during Hamlet's interview with Ophelia : he himself spies upon Hamlet's interview with his mother. It is impossible not to see that these things are made both futile and hateful in Polonius, and they *were* precisely the things that were detested in Cecil.

It is also worthy of note that Burleigh took the utmost care *not* to conduct marriage projects for his daughter in a way that might suggest he was using her to further his own interests.

" How careful he was to avoid all cause for doubt is seen by his answer to Lord Shrewsbury's offer of his son as a husband for one of Burleigh's daughters. . . . The match proposed was a good one and the Lord Treasurer—a new noble—was flattered and pleased by the offer." [1]

He refused it, however, because Shrewsbury was in charge of the Queen of Scots, and he feared the suspicion of intrigues.

" A similar but more flattering offer was made by the Earl

---

[1] Martin Hume.

of Essex in 1573 on behalf of his son ; but this also was declined."

Cecil, in fact, was always particularly careful not to let Elizabeth or anyone else think that ambition for his daughter could tempt him into unwise political plans.

In exactly the same way we find Polonius guarding himself against any suspicion that he may have encouraged Hamlet's advances to Ophelia. " The king asks [1] : " How hath she received his love ? " and Polonius enquires, " What do you think of me ? " The king replies : " As of a man faithful and honourable " ; Polonius proceeds to explain that, such being the case, he could not possibly have encouraged the love between Hamlet and his daughter ; but he had informed the latter that she must " lock herself " from the prince.

There is a further curious parallel in the fact that when Cecil's daughter—Elizabeth—married De Vere, Earl of Oxford—the husband turned sulky, separated himself from his wife, and declared that it was Cecil's fault for influencing his wife against him.

" A few days later Burghley had reason to be still more angry with Oxford himself, though with his reverence for rank he appears to have treated him with inexhaustible patience and forbearance. . . . Oxford declined to meet his wife or to hold any communication with her ; Burghley reasoned, remonstrated, and besought in vain. Oxford was sulky and intractable. His wife, he said, had been influenced by her parents against him and he would have nothing more to do with her."

---

[1] Act II., ii.

So, also, in the drama we find Polonius interfering between his daughter and her lover, we find his machinations so successful that Hamlet turns sulky, and is alienated from Ophelia for good.

Other significant details may be observed.

Cecil was a new man, and nothing annoyed him more than to have the fact called to his attention. " The most artful of his enemies, Father Persons, well knew the weak point in his armour, and wounded him to the quick in his books, in which he pretended to show that the Lord Treasurer was of base origin, his father a tavern-keeper, and he himself a bell-ringer. We have seen in a former case that attacks upon his ancestry almost alone aroused Lord Burleigh's anger." [1]

Hamlet, we may remember, taunts Polonius with following a base trade, with being a fishmonger; Polonius repudiates the idea with scorn, to which Hamlet retorts: " Then, I would you were so honest a man." [2]

There is probably more than one meaning here, but the most obvious is a taunt at a low origin.

Again Ophelia sings songs of lamentation one of which seems obviously intended for her father. " He is dead and gone"; she confuses him with a religious man: "his cockle hat and staff And his sandal shoon." [3]

Towards the end of Burleigh's life there was, apparently, a standing jest about him in the character of a religious man, a hermit.

Thus, Martin Hume refers to the queen's visit to Theobalds, and to a letter presented by a man dressed as a hermit; the letter reminded her that the last time

[1] Martin Hume.   [2] Act II., ii   [3] Act IV., v.

she came "his founder, upon a strange conceit, to feed his own humour, had placed the hermit contrary to his profession in his house, whilst he (Burghley) had retired to the hermit's poor cell."

Yet more curious parallels may be quoted. In a strange letter to Essex, Lord Henry Howard exults that "the dromedary that would have won the favour of the Queen of Sabez is almost enraged" (meaning Burleigh by the dromedary), and asks the earl whether "he cannot drag out the old leviathan and his cub" (meaning the two Cecils). We may surely compare this with Hamlet's conversation with Polonius :

HAM. Do you see yonder cloud that's almost in shape of a camel ?
POL. By the mass, and 'tis like a camel, indeed.
HAM. Methinks it is like a weasel.
POL. It is backed like a weasel.
HAM. Or like a whale ?
POL. Very like a whale.[1]

When we remember that Shakespeare would, in all human probability, have had access to the Essex correspondence shown by Essex himself, we can see the point still more strongly.

It is hardly necessary to show, how, in the correspondence of the time, such as that of Standen and Anthony Bacon, Burleigh is continually alluded to with contempt. Thus Standen writes to Anthony Bacon, March 1595, that the queen paid no heed to Burleigh, when he protested against the expedition to Cadiz : "When she saw it booted not to stay him, she said he was a ' froward old fool.' "

[1] Act III., ii.

Anthony, even in his correspondence with Lady Anne Bacon, refers to Burleigh continually as " the old man."

This is the general tone of Hamlet to Polonius. Burleigh seems to have done his utmost to conciliate Essex, and Anthony Bacon speaks of Burleigh's humiliation with pleasure : " Our Earl hath made the old Fox to crouch and whine." The humiliation of Burleigh by his scornful rival was, indeed, one of the standing jests of the court.

I may also quote in this connection Jonson's estimate of the character of Polonius :

" Polonius is a man bred in courts, exercised in business, stored with observation, confident in his knowledge, proud of his eloquence and declining into dotage, . . . This idea of dotage encroaching upon wisdom will solve all the phenomena of the character of Polonius."

Now, it does not seem to me possible that an Elizabethan audience could overlook the resemblances between Polonius and Burleigh, they are at once so wide and all-embracing and so minute and detailed.

We have the fact that each is a councillor, almost supreme in his office, isolated in his generation with no person of equal authority near him. Each has a passion for detail, for personal management, for analysing matters with the minutest care. Each has the habit of giving worldly-wise maxims to a son, maxims which are full of prudence but totally lacking in generosity and unselfishness, maxims which are sometimes almost word for word the same. Each has a spendthrift son, who goes to Paris and who receives many instructions from his father, a licentious son who is watched by his father's orders, and reports upon whom are brought home by the father's commands. Each takes the same care not to aim too high in a daughter's marriage lest he should compromise his own position. Each causes a separation between his daughter and the man she loves because the daughter is believed to be completely the father's agent and his decoy. Each has the same methods of statecraft, by intercepting letters of the most private nature, by shameless, undignified incessant spying, spying practised upon all possible occasions. Each has the same reverence for rank, the same interest in the university and university life, the same assumption of classical scholarship, the same dislike of quarrels, the same willingness to bear insults rather than resent them.

Each is insulted by being compared to various animals, a camel, a weasel, and a whale, on one side, a dromedary, a fox and a whale on the other. Each is made a public butt by a brilliant young man, by Hamlet in the one case, and by the Earl of Essex in the other.

It is difficult to see how Shakespeare could have got more resemblances into the brief space at his disposal. Add to this the fact that the Cecils were the bitter enemies of Essex and his party, that it was the son of Burleigh who has supposed to have triumphed over and destroyed the unhappy Essex, and we have a motive for Shakespeare's satire of the most powerful and cogent kind.

It does not seem to me particularly difficult to see what Shakespeare's method is. Burleigh was just precisely one of the characters who would interest his—

Shakespeare's—audience most, and who really did present a magnificent subject for study. On the other hand, from the dramatic point of view, Burleigh had one immense disadvantage : that nothing in particular had ever happened to him, and that he died quite respectably and tranquilly in his bed. The murder of Rizzio was, however, one of the most dramatic events in recorded history ; Shakespeare, therefore, combines the character of Burleigh with the end of Rizzio. The dramatic motive for doing so is just as clear and definite as the dramatic motive for combining the parts of the two Bothwells in one, and calling them both Claudius.

We have, of course, a real parallel between Rizzio and Cecil ; both were men put in a position of supreme trust and wielding immense power by secret and underhand methods ; both were regarded as unprincipled and intriguers, and both were objects of detestation and dislike.

Moreover, the uniting in one of the two characters stitches, as it were, the two parts of the drama together ; it brings the James I. part into close relation with the Essex part.

CHAPTER VI

OPHELIA

I WILL turn now to another portion of the play: that connected with Ophelia. Let us note at the outset three things:

(1) That there is an obvious dramatic motive for adding this love story to the play.

(2) That it can hardly have any relation to the history of James I.

(3) That it cannot fairly be said to be suggested by the saga source. I will deal with these points in order.

(1) The dramatic motive for the addition of Ophelia's story is plain enough; it adds greatly to the interest of *Hamlet* as a play, and to the interest of the prince himself as a character. Just as the addition of the story of Marguerite to that of *Faust* increases the value of the drama by adding pathos and tenderness to something that would otherwise be too purely intellectual, so does the addition of Ophelia's story increase by its pathos the value of *Hamlet*.

(2) Apparently, also, this portion of the play has nothing whatever to do with James I. James married, as most princes marry, in the same conventional and well-accepted way, and the only romantic circumstance connected with his marriage was the voyage to bring his bride home to Scotland, which has already been discussed.

I

(3) Neither does the saga give much suggestion. Saxo recounts how Amleth's enemies attempt to employ a certain woman as a decoy ; they plan that she shall entice the prince, who is pretending madness, to make love to her, and so obtain possession of his secrets ; Amleth, however, is forewarned by a friend who fastens a piece of straw to a horse-fly, and sends it past the place where Amleth lurks. Amleth detects the meaning of this somewhat fantastic device ; he drags the woman off into a remote covert where he violates her, but without revealing anything or betraying himself in any way at all. She is so deeply ashamed that she herself denies any connection between them, and the trap thus proves of no avail.

The Hystorie of Hamblet smooths out some of the worst absurdities from this narrative and says that the lady had " from her infancy loved and favoured him," but here also she is a mere decoy to vice, outwitted and rejected.

It is obvious that we are miles away from the story of Ophelia and Hamlet with all its romance and subtlety. What seems plausible is that the woman in the saga was the mere starting-point, and that all the rest is the poet's own creation. But here, again, let us refer to our standard criterion—the Elizabethan audience. Let us remember that the point from which we started was the Essex conspiracy and the Essex trial with which the subject of the Scottish succession was inseparably bound up.

Would the audience think the story of Ophelia had anything to do with the Essex trial ?

I can only say that I feel pretty sure they would, for it shows features which have the most marked resemblances to the stories of the two heroines connected with that trial: Elizabeth Vernon, the wife of Southampton, and Lady Essex.

If Shakespeare started from this point he would most certainly find there the suggestion for his love-story.

We may quote a letter from Rowland White:

" My lord of Southampton doth with *too much familiarity* court the fair Mistress Vernon, while his friends, observing the Queen's humours towards my Lord of Essex, do what they can to bring her to favour him, but in vain."

Southampton's love for Elizabeth Vernon cost him the favour of the queen; nothing would induce Elizabeth to consent to his marriage. From this time (1595) onwards Southampton's high spirit was incessantly galled; he was kept apart from the woman he loved, ordered to absent himself from Court, and continually checked in his public career.

We may quote the following extracts from Rowland White's letters January 14th, 1598:

" I hear my Lord of Southampton goes with Mr Secretary to France, and so onward on his travels, which course of his doth extremely grieve his mistress, that passes her time in weeping and lamenting."

And again on February 1st:

" My Lord of Southampton is much troubled by her Majesty's strangest usage of him. Somebody hath played unfriendly parts with him. Mr Secretary hath procured him license to travel. *His fair mistress* doth wash her fairest face with many tears. *I pray God his going away bring her to no such infirmity which is as it were hereditary to her name.*" February 12th, "My Lord of Southampton is gone and hath left behind him a fair gentlewoman that hath almost wept out her fairest eyes."

Shortly after Elizabeth Vernon was ordered away from Court, Chamberlain writes:

"Mrs Vernon is from the Court and lies at Essex House. Some say she hath taken a *venue* under her girdle and swells upon it; yet she complains not of *foul play* but says My Lord of Southampton will justify it, and it is bruited underhand that he was lately here four days in great secret of purpose to marry her and effected it accordingly."

The secret marriage seems to have taken place in 1598, and the queen, possibly getting to hear of it, was totally alienated from Southampton.

In 1599, Essex went to Ireland; that Shakespeare watched this venture with interest and hoped for a successful issue is proved by the open and daring reference to it in *Henry V*. Southampton accompanied Essex, and was made his General of Horse, but the queen commanded Essex to revoke the appointment. Southampton returned to London, and continued to give great offence by absenting himself from Court and frequenting plays instead. White writes on October 19th: "My Lord Southampton and Lord Rutland come not to Court, they pass away the time in London *merely in going to plays every day.*"

The offence in this lay, of course, in the connection the stage was invariably supposed to have with politics.

Both Essex and Southampton repeatedly offended

the queen by the connection they had with plays and players, just as Hamlet offended the king by *his* connection with plays and players; if Elizabethan dramas in general, and Shakespeare's in particular, were always dealing with purely imaginary events and characters where would be the cause for the annoyance?

The candid truth is, all our evidence goes to show that the dramatists in general, *and Shakespeare quite as much as the others*, offended as Hamlet did in the Gonzago play.

Southampton, as we have already pointed out, in disgrace at the Court, joined in the rash and foolish Essex conspiracy. Like Essex, he was condemned to death, but the sentence was commuted to perpetual imprisonment; this was the situation in which he lay at the time *Hamlet* was written, and Southampton's only hope lay in the accession of James I.; as the Essex conspiracy was supposed to be in his favour, James might naturally be expected to set Southampton free and, as a matter of fact, it was one of the first things he did on his progress in April 1603. Chamberlain says:

" the 10th of this month the Earl of Southampton was delivered out of the Tower, and the King looked upon him with a smiling countenance. . . . These bountiful beginnings raise all men's spirits and put them in great hopes."

Now, we can surely see a certain resemblance between these events and the love-story of Hamlet and Ophelia. There is, to begin with, the wooing with *too much familiarity*.

Polonius and Laertes both complain to Ophelia that

she is laying her honour too much open to suspicion.
Laertes says :

> " weigh what loss your honour may sustain
> If with too credent ear you list his songs,
> Or lose your heart, or your chaste treasure open
> To his unmaster'd importunity." [1]

Polonius adds :

> 'Tis told me, he hath very oft of late
> Given private time to you ; and you yourself
> Have of your audience been most free and bounteous . . .
> You do not understand yourself so clearly
> As it behoves my daughter and your honour."

Elizabeth Vernon, when her honour was called in
question, justified herself and her lover by declaring
that he had pledged her his word; so Ophelia justifies
herself and Hamlet :

> " He hath importuned me with love
> In honourable fashion . . .
> And hath given countenance to his speech, my lord,
> With almost all the holy vows of heaven."

Elizabeth Vernon is separated from her lover, and so
is Ophelia :

> . . . " This is for all:
> I would not, in plain terms, from this time forth
> Have you so slander any moment leisure
> As to give words or talk with the Lord Hamlet."

Elizabeth Vernon's love affair was made a court affair
and a matter of state interference; it was discussed by
everyone in a way calculated to cause agony to a sensitive
soul : so is Ophelia's.

Since marriage was made impossible by this cruel
interference there was a very strong suspicion that

[1] Act I., iii.

Elizabeth Vernon had been seduced; her lover went away, and in his absence she was in the deepest distress and in danger of insanity. All these things unite to make pathetic the story of Ophelia: she is under the shadow of disgrace; Hamlet's language to her in the play scene is of the coarsest and most imprudent kind, and such as would destroy her reputation in the ears of anyone overhearing it; the songs she herself sings in her madness suggest the same thing. Does it not look as if Shakespeare were simply carrying a step farther, and making a degree more pathetic, the events already suggested to him by his friend's story? At any rate, the play is here, also, far and away closer to contemporary events that it is to its so-called sources.

Southampton, certainly the poet's generous patron, quite possibly his best-beloved friend, was even then in the Tower, his neck in jeopardy on account of the peril brought about by this very love-story. He and his mistress were regarded as innocent unhappy beings, exasperated into disgrace by the needless persecution of a true love.

Could anything be more plausible than that Shakespeare would himself be deeply and profoundly moved by their fate, and would desire to awaken sympathy with them if he could? And, if to show his sympathy also perfects his wonderful drama, why not?

Moreover, the unity which he must consider first and foremost, is already a unity in the minds of his audience, for all these things were bound up in the most intimate and vital way with the questions of the Essex conspiracy and the Scottish Succession.

With regard to the relations between Hamlet and
Ophelia there can be little doubt, I think, that
Shakespeare means them to be substantially innocent
since they are depicted with so much sympathy;
but whether they were meant to be innocent in the
literal sense of the word is quite another question.
We must not allow ourselves to be misled by Victorian
prudery.

The suspicions of Laertes and Polonius might be explained to be due to their own foulness of mind; but
Hamlet suggests the same thing by his language in the
play scene, and so does Ophelia in her songs—all these
things taken together imply a conclusion other than that
of innocence.

May it not be an essential part of Hamlet's tragedy
that he and the woman he loves have genuinely yielded
to temptation?

In this connection I may quote Tieck:

" How much of fine observation is there in what is said of
Ophelia in Goethe's ' Wilhelm Meister ': But, if I do not
entirely misunderstand Shakespeare, the poet has meant to
intimate throughout the piece that the poor girl, in the
ardour of her passion for the fair prince, has yielded all to
him. The hints and warnings of Laertes come too late. It
is tender and worthy of the great poet to leave the relation
of Hamlet and Ophelia, like much else in the piece, a riddle ;
but it is from this point of view alone that Hamlet's behaviour,
his bitterness and Ophelia's suffering and madness, find
connection and consistency."

" At the acting of the play before the court, Ophelia has
to endure all sorts of coarseness from Hamlet before all the
courtiers ; he treats her without that respect which she
appears to him to have long before forfeited."

I cannot help adding that our modern habit of sentimental interpretation interferes with Shakespeare's tragedy ; if the worst happened to Ophelia it does not make her tragedy less, but only more poignant ; it makes her as overwhelmingly pathetic as Marguerite in *Faust*.

In this connection I may point out that many critics have been puzzled by the fact that Hamlet's love for Ophelia seems to be obvious only in certain scenes of the play and not in others.

Furnivall goes so far as to think that the Hamlet who was at first depicted as the lover of Ophelia was very different and not as mature as the later Hamlet :

" I look on it as certain that when Shakespeare began the play he conceived Hamlet as quite a young man. But, as the play grew, as greater weight of reflection, of insight into character, of knowledge of life, etc., was wanted, Shakespeare necessarily and naturally made Hamlet a formed man ; and by the time that he got to the grave-digger's scene, told us the prince was thirty—the right age for him, but not his age when Laertes and Polonius warned Ophelia against his blood that burned in youthful fancy for her—" a toy in the blood." The two parts of the play are inconsistent on this main point in Hamlet's state."

Now, this is exactly my own point of view, only I think the discrepancy arises from the fact that Shakespeare is drawing his Hamlet from more than one original, that the character is, in fact, a composite, and that all the parts of the composite are not consistent.

Another point to be noted, is that Hamlet never refers to Ophelia in his soliloquies ; in these soliloquies he shows himself a good deal of a misogynist and his misogyny appears to be largely due to his mother's misconduct, but he never refers either to Ophelia's love for him, or to his for her ; in fact, he forgets all about her during the greater part of the play. This is very curious if he really cared for her so deeply.

Another detail to observe lies in one of the songs sung by Ophelia ; it is a lascivious song, and concerns the meeting of two lovers as Valentines and their licentious union ; Nash wrote for Southampton a lascivious poem entitled " The Choosing of Valentines " which deals with almost identical circumstances ; it was dedicated to the earl in two sonnets, one prefixed and the other suffixed.

CHAPTER VII

HAMLET AND ESSEX

I WILL return now to the point from which I started—the Essex trial—for it seems to me obvious that the character of Hamlet and the experiences of Hamlet include, also, a good deal suggested by Essex.

Essex, we may remember, had a side of his character which was deeply studious and by nature he was a student and a soldier far more than a courtier. Francis Bacon advised him to appear "bookish and contemplative." [1] In his *Apology* addressed to Anthony Bacon, Essex says :

" For my infection in nature, it was indifferent to books and arms and was more inflamed with the love of knowledge than with the love of fame. . . . Witness your rarely qualified brother . . . and my bookishness from my very childhood."

Wotton, in his *Reliquiæ*, gives testimony to the same effect :

" It is certain that he (Leicester) drew him (Essex) first into the fatal circle from a kind of resolved privateness at his house at Lampsie in South Wales when, after the academical life, he had taken such a taste for the rural as I have heard him say . . . he could have well bent his mind to a retired course."

---

[1] Abbot, *Bacon and Essex.*

Now, here we surely see the parallel with Hamlet in the studious nature which loves retirement, and wishes to avoid the court and to live in seclusion after the university course.

" Essex," says Mr Abbott, "sorely needed guidance, and, unlike many of the guideless, he knew that he needed it. Like Hamlet he was and knew that he was too liable to be ' passion's slave ' and he longed for some calm, steadfast and philosophic Horatio. . . .   Physically and mentally Essex was as unstable as Hamlet . . . at one time outshining all his peers in the glory of the tilt-yard, at the next, sulking in solitude at Wanstead ; now the Queen's chief councillor and sole depositary of all state secrets, now again forswearing all work, neglecting all his own interests and even those of his friends ; at one moment exulting . . . at another exclaiming ' Vanitas vanitatum ' and despairing even of honour and safety. . . .   His instability more often injured himself than his friends."

Just as Essex had come reluctantly to Court from his studies, so he often desired to retire from it, and at times did so.   In a letter to Lady Anne Bacon, the Earl complains : " I live in a place where I am hourly compassed against and practised upon."

Anthony Bacon accuses Cecil of tampering with his correspondence, and Essex feels ill at ease amid all this intrigue, and once more resorts to his old expedient of absenting himself from Court.

" Essex," says Mr Abbott, " was during the last years of his life, continually suffering from melancholy."

Essex, also, seemed at times on the verge of insanity. " The Earl is crazed," writes Chamberlain, " but whether more in mind or body, is doubtful."

At his trial Essex was accused by Robert Cecil of ambition, and of aspiring to the Crown:

" I have said the King of Scots was a competitor; and you I have said are a Competitor; you would depose the Queen, you would be King of England, and call a Parliament."

Essex, in his reply, dwelt on his lack of ambition:

" I have laboured and by my prayers to God earnestly desired that I might be armed with patience to endure all afflictions. . . . God which knoweth the secrets of all hearts knows that I never sought the Crown of England, nor ever wished to be a higher degree than that of subject."

Now, I have already pointed out, that in the original saga, one of Hamlet's chief motives was his desire to gain the crown for himself; in Shakespeare's play this is entirely omitted, and the hero is characterised by a complete lack of ambition, very curious in his situation, but explicable enough if Shakespeare is taking hints from somebody against whom ambition had been made a criminal charge.

Speaking of the last two years of Essex's life, Mr Abbott says:

" There can be no question at all that, rightly or wrongly, Essex believed that his enemies around the Queen's person were plotting the betrayal of his country as well as the ruin of himself and also that in his moods of depression and melancholy, he thought his life to be in immediate danger."

" He was at this time given to fits of gloom and despair."

Harrington says of him in such a mood " the man's soul tosseth to and fro like a troubled sea."

" His irresolution," says Mr Abbott again, " bordered on the fitfulness of insanity."

Now here, once more, we surely have remarkable parallels to Hamlet : in the last part of the play we have Hamlet's feeling that his enemies are plotting his death, and will certainly achieve it: we have his premonition, " But thou wouldst not think, how ill all's here about my heart." [1]

The mind " tossing like a troubled sea," reminds us of Hamlet's own metaphor " to take arms against a sea of troubles, And by opposing end them." [2]

Essex, in fact, in the last year of his life, was, as Mr Abbott so justly points out, startlingly like Hamlet : he was irresolute almost to the point of insanity, he was surrounded by cunning enemies who plotted against his life, he had a premonition of disaster.

Essex, moreover, suffered from a misery so great that he often longed for death. Thus he said at his trial :

" I will not (I protest to God) speak to save my life ; for those that persecute it against me, shall do me a good turn to rid me of much misery and themselves of fear."

We may compare this with Hamlet. [3]

> " To die : to sleep ;
> No more ; and by a sleep to say we end
> The heart-ache, and the thousand natural shocks
> That flesh is heir to, 'tis a consummation
> Devoutly to be wished."

Essex, on being condemned, said, as he had often done during his trial : " My own life I do not value," but he besought mercy for the Earl of Southampton.

---

[1] Act V., ii.   [2] Act III., i.   [3] Act III., i.

We may compare Hamlet, " I do not set my life at a pin's fee." [1]

Again Essex said, " I protest I do crave her Majesty's mercy with all humility ; yet I had rather die than live in misery."

We have Hamlet's [2] :

" For who would bear the whips and scorns of time
 The oppressor's wrong, the proud man's contumely, . . .
 When he himself might his quietus make
 With a bare bodkin."

Essex, on hearing his sentence, said : " My Lord, I am not at all dismayed to receive this sentence, for death is far more cheerful to me than life ; and I shall die as cheerful a death as ever man did."

Essex, in fact, showed emphatically during the last period of his life, the world-weariness and the life-weariness which we associate so markedly with Hamlet.

John Chamberlain, writing February 21st, 1600-1, says :

" The Earl of Essex announced that he was driven to do what he did for safety of his life. . . . This was the summe of his answer, but delivered with such bravery and so many words that a man might easily perceive that, as he had ever lived popularly, so his chief care was to have a good opinion in the people's minds now at parting."

We may compare this with Hamlet's intense anxiety not to leave after him " a wounded name," and his injunction to Horatio to " tell my story." [3]

[1] Act I., iv.　　[2] Act III., i.　　[3] Act V., ii.

Malone pointed out long ago that Shakespeare in writing the last words of Horatio's farewell :

> " Now cracks a noble heart—Good night, sweet prince,
>   And flights of Angels sing thee to thy rest,"

had in his mind the last words of Essex in his prayer on the scaffold: "And when my soul and body shall part, *send thy blessed angels to be near unto me which may convey it to the joys of heaven.*" We may also note that shortly after the execution there was a ballad published, entitled *Essex' Last Good-night.* It is a rough and doggerel production and every verse ends with the refrain of "good night."

> " He never yet hurt Mother's son,
>   His quarrel still maintains the right,
>   Which the tears my face down run
>   When I think on his last Good-Night."
>   .   .   .   .   .
> " And life shall make amends for all
>   For Essex bids the world ' Good-Night.' "

It looks as if Shakespeare were remembering and reminding his audience of both.

The whole part of Hamlet which is concerned with the players seems to me to have, in all probability, a great deal to do with Essex.

Both Essex and Southampton gave repeated offence to the queen by the way in which they associated themselves with actors and stage plays.

Mr Ingram says :

"At that time the Stage, to a great extent, possessed the influence which in a later age passed to the Press. Having no daily journals or other accessible means of rapid and general communication on topics of common interest, the public looked to and found what it wanted in the Stage. The play supplied references to the political, religious and social events of the day. Writers and players found their profit in responding to the popular feeling of their audience, and although many times fine and imprisonment rewarded their attempt to meddle with matters of state, they persisted in their efforts." [1]

Now it has already been pointed out that Shakespeare's company had the closest possible connection with the Essex trial through their repeated performance of *Richard II.*, and that his connection with the play told heavily against Essex at the trial itself since the deposition scene and the death were taken as being an earnest of what he intended to do with the queen.

The reader will also remember that one of the chief counts in the indictment against Essex was his patronage of Haywarde's book on Henry IV., which was supposed to contain numerous references to Elizabeth's favouritism and other objectionable features of her reign.

Now surely we can see here many parallels with Hamlet. We see Hamlet treating the players with the utmost courtesy, on terms of familiarity with them, interested in their art, giving them instructions and consulting with them as to the plays they are to perform ; his connection with them is regarded with great suspicion by Polonius and the king (exactly as the queen objected to Essex an Scuthampton having a connection with the players), and with justice, for Hamlet does use them for political purposes exactly as Essex had used them for political purposes.

[1] *Christopher Marlowe and his Associates.*

K

Hamlet's method of dealing with the Gonzago play is exactly the method which Shakespeare had been accused of employing both in *Henry IV.* and *Richard II.* It seems to me, as I have said before, exceedingly probable that it was the method he used in dealing with *Hamlet*. He selects a story which shows a considerable likeness to the murder of his father, he accentuates that likeness, and makes it more pointed, and then, when the king is naturally full of indignation, he leaps to his feet and cries that " the story is extant," and " in choice Italian." This is probably the exact method by which Shakespeare and his fellows evaded the censor.

Hamlet himself describes the players, as " the abstract and brief chronicles of the time: after your death you were better have a bad epitaph than their ill report while you live."[1]   Now, in what sense could they be " the abstract and brief chronicles of the time," if their plays dealt with bronze-age Britain, with ancient Denmark and remote Illyria, and with *nothing* else.

Moreover, if this were the case, why should the Star Chamber concern itself so closely with both dramatists and actors. The truth is that we have overwhelming evidence for the *political* influence of the stage, and Shakespeare and Shakespeare's company were as deeply involved as anyone.

In the case of Hamlet his meddling with the Gonzago play is the thing that excites the suspicion of the king, which never afterwards slumbered ; he places his neck in jeopardy, and ultimately brings his fate upon him through this play.   In exactly the same way did Essex

[1] Act II., ii.

place his neck in jeopardy, and help to bring suspicion upon himself (as his trial shows) by his connection with *Richard II*.

All this part of *Hamlet* is quite obviously full of topical allusions, for Shakespeare even makes a reference to the boys, the "little eyases" who supplanted himself and his company in the favour of the court when they were disgraced on account of this very affair.

There can be little doubt that Shakespeare brings his own company in here. Hamlet asks: "What players are they?"

> Ros. Even those you were wont to take delight in, the tragedians of the city.
> HAM. How chances it they travel? their residence, both in reputation and profit, was better both ways.
> Ros. I think their inhibition comes by the means of the late innovation.
> HAM. Do they hold the same estimation they did when I was in the city? are they so followed?
> Ros. No, indeed, they are not.
> HAM. How comes it? do they grow rusty?
> Ros. Nay, their endeavour keeps in the wonted pace; but there is, sir, an aery of children, little eyases, that cry out on the top of question and are most tyrannically clapped for't."

Now, this is one of the passages quite definitely accepted by Mr Boas and others as referring to Shakespeare's own company, and one of the passages they mainly rely upon in estimating the date of the play. But, if Shakespeare inserts his company like this into the very middle of *Hamlet*, what is there to prevent him from inserting also the method of himself and his company into the midst of *Hamlet*, and explaining it in the Gonzago play?

Can we, as a matter of fact, imagine a better method of doing it, and of suggesting that *Hamlet is* full of historical parallels even though the story *is* extant already as a play.

Another portion of *Hamlet* which seems to me to contain, in all probability, reference to Essex, is the Laertes story.   There is certainly no parallel whatever to this in the original saga, but there is in the last years of the life of Essex.

Laertes is cunningly used by Claudius as a rival to Hamlet; he tries to destroy them by pitting them one against the other.

It was in exactly the same way that Raleigh had been pitted against Essex.   Mr Innes[1] says :

" Old Lord Burleigh died, and a considerable portion of the story of the Queen's last years is really the story of the crafty intriguing by which Robert Cecil first urged Essex to the ruin on which he was ready enough to rush, and then laid his mines for the destruction of Raleigh while carefully avoiding the odium in both cases."

Essex repeatedly stated at the time of his abortive attempt, and also during his trial, that he believed his life in danger, and that Raleigh and others had been appointed to assassinate him.

Anthony Weldon states that the destruction of Essex was always counted against Robert Cecil :

" Sir Robert Cecil was a very wise man, but much hated in England by reason of the fresh bleeding of that unusually beloved Earl of Essex."

---

[1] "Walter Raleigh " (in *Ten Tudor Statesmen*).

At the Essex trial Masham deposed, February 10th, 1601 :

> " I heard that Lord Essex should have been murdered, and was come guarded into London for safety. . . . I met a servant of Lady Essex who told me that Cobham and Raleigh would have murdered my lord that night. . . . My lord came forth himself and declared to the people that he should have been murdered and came to them for safety. . . . "

So, in *Hamlet*, Claudius tries to employ Laertes to get rid of Hamlet in order to avoid the odium himself ; the method to be employed is that of an " envenomed foil " ; now, venom is, of course, an ever-recurring metaphor for slander, and stabbing was the exact method of death expected by Essex himself.

On March 3rd, 1601, the deposition of Masham was confirmed by that of Dr Fletcher : Mr Temple said that the Earl was waylaid by Sir Walter Raleigh and his company of ruffians, and that if he went (*i.e.* to court), he should certainly be martyred. That he (Temple) acquainted me and others of my Lord's friends with it, that they might know how he was pursued by his enemies, meaning Sir Walter Raleigh and his company.

We may remember in this connection that Raleigh was present at the death of Essex, but, for fear lest he might be accused of triumphing over him he withdrew to some distance, and saw it from the armoury only.

Raleigh is said to have shed tears of compassion. During all the remainder of his life he was concerned to excuse himself from complicity.

Even at his death (1618), it was the charge against

him that he thought most grievous ; on the scaffold Raleigh entreated everyone to believe

"that he had not been instrumental in causing the death of the Earl of Essex nor had he rejoiced thereat, as had been imported to him. On the contrary he had regretted it more than his own sins."

Here, again, it is impossible not to see the parallel with Hamlet.

Hamlet was written when it was still believed that Raleigh had been instrumental in the destruction of Essex ; but it was also believed that his deed was scarcely consummated before he had felt remorse. This is the exact situation of Laertes, who realises too late how he has been practised upon :

> " Hamlet ; Hamlet, thou art slain ;
> No medicine in the world can do thee good :
> In thee there is not half an hour of life,
> The treacherous instrument is in thy hand,
> Unbated and envenomed."

Sir Anthony Weldon states that it was resentment for the death of Essex which caused James, on his accession, to be so hard on Raleigh.

It is probable also that the grave-digging scene owes something to the execution of Essex. It certainly owes nothing to the original saga ; in the saga Amleth returns from Britain to Jutland, and finds the court celebrating his own funeral :

" Covered with filth, he entered the banquet room where obsequies were being held and struck all men utterly aghast, rumour having falsely noised about his death.

Before the court can recover from its astonishment Amleth gets the better of them all, and burns them to death in the banqueting hall. This is also the situation in the *Historie of Hamblet*.

It seems possible that this feigned funeral of Hamlet may have suggested the real funeral of Ophelia; but the conception of the grave-diggers owes much more to contemporary events. Essex was so generally beloved that the ordinary executioner refused his task; a stranger had to be found to behead the Earl, and the man bungled his task and performed it horribly; the anger of the populace against him was so great that he dared not appear in the streets of London for fear of being lynched.

Edmond Howes's continuation of Stow's *Chronicle* states;

"The 25 of February, being Ash-wednesday, about 8. of the clocke in the morning was the sentence of death executed upon Robert Devereux earle of Essex, within the Tower of London. . . . The hangman was beaten as hee returned thence, so that the sheriffes of London were called to assist and rescue him from such as would have murthered him."

Now in *Hamlet* the chief point of the grave-digging scene is the way in which the " knave " insults the remains of the dead, and the immense helplessness of the dead before these insults. The " knave " cares nothing for the skulls, " he jowls " one to the ground as " if it were Cain's jawbone that did the first murder." He knocks another about the mazzard with his spade. It has been usual to explain the incident of Yorick's skull as referring to the recent death of Tarleton, the great comedian of Shakespeare's company: it may be so; but it is much

more probable that the incident refers to Essex ; Tarleton
was certainly not executed, and no one has ever told us
that his dead body was insulted, whereas Yorick's skull
must be severed from his body, since Hamlet takes it
in his hands.   Moreover, Yorick's skull is certainly insulted ; as acted on the stage the clown usually strikes
it as he strikes the others.   Yorick is described as the
" king's jester," " a fellow of infinite jest," " of most
excellent fancy " ;   and Essex had been one of the most
brilliant and the wittiest of all the courtiers.

Take, moreover, the language in which Hamlet
addresses the skull when he says : " Get you to my lady's
amber, and tell her, let her paint an inch thick, to this
favour she must come ; make her laugh at that."

This surely has no suggestion of Tarleton ; but it is
most gruesome and terrible if it applies to Essex ; it
reminds us of the famous incident when, on his return
from Ireland, Essex rushed into the presence of his
queen, and found her at her toilet—probably dishevelled
and painting, an incident which was supposed to have
had a most untoward effect upon his fate.   An imagination worthy of Dante to make the skull of the victim
interrupt once again at the toilette !

Here, also, we probably find the reason for comparing
the skull to that of Alexander's.   Where would be the
point of comparing Tarleton's skull to Alexander's, or
his dust to that of " imperious Cæsar " ; but there is
real point in comparing that of Essex, for Essex had been
one of the most daring and brilliant soldiers of his day.
The exploit of Essex against Cadiz was a most brilliant
feat of arms in which, like Alexander, he had ventured

almost single-handed, into a hostile city ; like Alexander, Essex had travelled widely, and met his enemies in distant lands and, like him, he too perished in his youth. Rashness was the quality of both, rashness and brilliance and an early death. Hamlet compares Yorick's skull to Alexander's : " Dost thou think Alexander looked o' this fashion i' the earth ? " and again, " Why may not imagination trace the noble dust of Alexander, till he find it stopping a bung-hole."

" Essex," says Mr Abbott, " was acknowledged, though on insufficient grounds no doubt, to be the ablest general in England ; it was precisely because he was acknowledged to be the ablest general that he was sent to Ireland."

We may compare, also, the contemporary pamphlet, *Honour in Perfection*, by G. M., usually attributed to Gervase Marklam, which deals with the house of Essex :

" The noble world is but a Theatre of Renoune, the Tongues of all people make up but the Trumpet which speaks them, and it is Eternitie itself which shall keep them unto everlasting memorie."

Moreover, Essex himself had been haunted by the dread of ignominy to his body if he died the death of a traitor, and had repeatedly spoken of it ; even before he came into open revolt he had been conscious of exposure to low-minded insults.

I quote the most pertinent extracts ; thus, in a letter written to the queen dated May 20th, 1600, Essex says of himself that he feels

" as if I were thrown into a corner like a dead carcass, I am gnawed upon and torn by the basest and vilest creatures upon earth.   The tavern-haunter speaks of me what he lists. Already they print me and make me speak to the world, and shortly they will print me in what forms they list upon the stage." [1]

Now, surely we have here remarkable parallels to the grave-digging scene ; Yorick's skull is thrown into a corner, it is " gnawed upon " by the vilest of creatures ; the clown is a tavern-haunter, for he sends his boy for a "stoup of liquor " even over his work, thus bringing the dead insulted bodies into the closest connection with the tavern.

Moreover, as we see, Essex was confident that he would be represented on the stage and, if so, why might not Shakespeare represent him and defend him ?

Shakespeare might have seen this very letter before it was sent ; there is no reason why he should not.

On receiving sentence, Essex said :

" And I think it fitting that my poor quarters, which have done her Majesty true service in divers parts of the world, should now at last be sacrificed and disposed of at her Majesty's pleasure."

Compare this with Hamlet's bitter irony :

" Imperious Cæsar, dead and turned to clay,
   Might stop a hole to keep the wind away." [2]

We may compare the declaration of the treasons uttered by a certain Abraham Colfe referring to Essex [3] :

" He commended a great general of the wars lately dead whom he called Veri Dux, extolling most highly his infancy, young years, and man's age, his embracing of learned men

---

[1] Birch, *Memoirs of Queen Elizabeth.*
[2] Act V., i.   [3] *State Papers*, 1601.

and warriors, who all followed him without pay. He named the journey to Cadiz, his forwardness there and felicity, and how men looked on his returning " tanquam in solem occidentum." . . . After his coming home he was " pessime tractatus, quia cum esset imperator imperata non fecerit," . . . His virtue which drew upon him the envy of great personages was the cause of his overthrow.

" . . . His enemies accused him of aspiring to a kingdom. . . . He showed how the executioners had three strokes at his head, that his very enemies could not choose but weep when they saw his head cut off. . . . His conclusion was, " You have heard of the life and death of a worthy general."

Surely, we have here the same train of thought as in Shakespeare ; the insulted dead, the shamed and humiliated dust and the " great general," so great that he is compared to an emperor and the leader of his country. History does not record that the dust of Alexander " stopped a bung-hole," or that the dust of Cæsar " patched a hole to expel the winter's flaw " ; but profound humiliation certainly happened to the dust of Essex.

Remember that the execution of Essex was still the grief of the whole country when *Hamlet* was played, and let us ask ourselves what Shakespeare's audience would be likely to think.

Another point to notice is that, before his death, Essex most passionately desired reconciliation with those whom he had esteemed his enemies. He professed to bear no malice to Lord Cobham and Sir Walter Raleigh and, as already quoted,[1] the latter is said to have shed tears when he witnessed the execution of Essex.

[1] Birch, *Memoirs of Queen Elizabeth.*

We may compare the reconciliation of Hamlet and Laertes.

> " Exchange forgiveness with me, noble Hamlet ;
>   Mine and my father's death come not upon thee,
>   Nor thine on me,"

and Hamlet's reply :

> " Heaven make thee free of it." [1]

Laertes is stabbed by the " envenomed foil " prepared for Hamlet, and, as he himself says :

> " I am justly kill'd with mine own treachery."

So was Raleigh destroyed by the same methods of slander which he had himself employed against Essex.

I turn now to an incident which has always puzzled commentators : the fight between Hamlet and Laertes in the grave.

Campbell points out that Hamlet's love for Ophelia only seems to occur in certain portions of the play and that, for instance, the burial scene seems to show an almost complete absence of it :

" Had it been in the mind of Shakespeare to show Hamlet in the agony of hopeless despair he must at that moment have been, had Ophelia been all in all to him . . . is there in all his writings so utter a failure in the attempt to give vent to an overwhelming passion ? . . . It seems not a little unaccountable that Hamlet should have been so slightly affected by her death."

Campbell points out that Hamlet's real motive in leaping into the grave appears to be, not love for Ophelia

[1] Act V., ii.

at all, but rivalry with Laertes—a very different passion. Campbell continues :

" When Hamlet leaps into the grave do we see in that any power of love ? I am sorry to confess that to me the whole of that scene is merely painful. It is anger with Laertes, not love for Ophelia, that makes Hamlet leap into the grave. Laertes' conduct, he tells us afterwards, put him into a towering passion—a state of mind which it is not easy to reconcile with any kind of sorrow for the dead Ophelia. But had he been attempting to describe the behaviour of an impassioned lover at the grave of his beloved I should be compelled to feel that he had not merely departed from nature, but that he had offered her the most profane violation and insult."

It seems to me that this fight in the grave may perhaps be best interpreted as symbolic. The whole Elizabethan age was passing away ; its glories were decaying and most of its great men were already dead ; of those who remained, the most distinguished—Essex and Raleigh— were flying at each other's throats, eager to destroy each other ; their queen was the shadow of herself, anyone knew she might die at any moment, and it was precisely over the question of her succession that the most violent quarrels broke out. The clown when first asked for whom the grave was made replies that it is for no man or no woman neither, and a little later on explains : " One that was a woman, sir, but, rest her soul, she's dead." It may be meant to symbolise the burial of a whole age. Hamlet and Laertes both profess that their motive for the quarrel in the grave is their love for Ophelia, and they " outface " each other in their professions of affection to her, the result being this disgraceful insult to her memory. Surely if it is meant as a symbol it is terribly appropriate, the last great Elizabethans destroying each other over the very body of their mistress, all the time professing their love, and a crafty enemy taking advantage of their quarrel to destroy them both. I can see no reason why Shakespeare should not introduce, at least, an element of symbolism into his plays ; the greatest of his predecessors—Spenser—wrote a poem which is one mass of symbolism ; symbolism was one of the chief methods in the religious drama which preceded Shakespeare's, and in one of his chief dramatic predecessors—Lyly.

Another scene which may possibly have been suggested by the Essex story is the casket scene between Hamlet and Ophelia when Ophelia returns the casket of his letters, declaring that they were love letters, and Hamlet is immediately enraged, and suspects her honesty.

We learn from the *State Papers*,[1] that the Countess of Essex had been used as an instrument to betray her husband. In June 1601, there was a long examination in the Star Chamber concerning a casket of letters which the Countess of Essex had entrusted to a certain Jane Daniells who had also been her gentlewoman.

" Jane's husband stole a number of the letters to have them copied. . . .

"The countess was greatly afraid that the Earl would be angry with her for suffering his long and passionate love-letters to be spread abroad . . . she swore they were not dangerous. . . . Daniells demanded three thousand pounds to give them back and the Countess was forced to sell her jewels. . . .

"At the time of the Earl's arraignment he pretended that

---

[1] Ed. Green.

the aforementioned letters had been stolen and counterfeited
by his adversaries. . . .

"The Court, pitying the Countess, . . . cleared her from all
suspicion of any ill intention towards her late husband."

Here, again, we surely have close parallels. Hamlet's
love-letters to Ophelia are intercepted and stolen ;
Hamlet asserts that he never gave her anything, while
she asserts that he did, but that the gifts were love-letters
and jewels ; moreover, this very casket scene is used
as a means to decoy Hamlet into the hands of his enemies,
and Ophelia is the innocent and unwilling instrument,
overwhelmed with distress by Hamlet's anger.

The parallel is, once again, suspiciously close, and this
also is a scene which has no parallel whatever in the
so-called literary source.

We may observe that Ophelia's description of her
lover stands out sharply from the Hamlet of much of
the play, the Hamlet who resembles James I., though
Ophelia's description of her lover would serve admirably for the Earl of Essex. She expressly tells us that
the Hamlet she had loved was both a " courtier " and
" a soldier."

> " O, what a noble mind is here o'erthrown !
>   The courtier's, soldier's, scholar's, eye, tongue, sword :
>   The expectancy and rose of the fair state.
>   The glass of fashion and the mould of form,
>   The observed of all observers, quite, quite, down ! "

When was the Hamlet of the rest of the play a soldier ?
Does he not expressly dislike bloodshed ?

How can he have been a courtier when he so ex-

pressly despises all the tricks of courtiers ?   How can
he have been the " glass of fashion," and the " mould
of form," when he thoroughly despised dress and
habiliments ?

How can he have been the " observed of all observers ? " when he shrank from notice, and desired
the privacy of study ?   How can he have been " un-
matched in form and feature " when, according to his
own mother, he was " fat and scant of breath."
Ophelia's lover is so different from the Hamlet of
most of the play as to suggest that he really was a
different person, which is confirmed by the fact that
this Hamlet forgets all about her, and never even refers
to her in his soliloquies.

Mr Bradley gives an admirable summary of this curious
indifference from which I quote a portion :

(1) How is it that, in his first soliloquy, Hamlet makes
no reference whatever to Ophelia ?

(2) How is it that, in his second soliloquy, on the
departure of the ghost, he again says nothing about her ?

.   .   .   .   .   .

(5) In what way are Hamlet's insults to Ophelia at
the play scene necessary either to his purpose of convincing her of his insanity or to his purpose of revenge ?

(6) How is it that neither when he kills Polonius,
nor afterwards, does he reflect that he has killed
Ophelia's father, or what the effect on Ophelia is likely
to be ?

(7) . . . there is no reference to Ophelia in the soliloquies of the first act, nor in those of any of the other
acts.

(8) In speaking to Horatio, Hamlet never mentions Ophelia, and at his death he says nothing of her.

It seems to me that these facts are practically impossible to explain if *Hamlet* is to be interpreted as psychology ; but if it is to be interpreted as mainly historical they are simple enough. We may compare with Ophelia's description of her lover, the description of Essex appended to the account of his trial in 1649 :

" There sleeps great Essex, darling of Mankind,
   Fair Honour's lamp, foul envie's prey, Art's fame,
   Nature's pride, Virtue's bulwark, lure of Mind,
   Wisdom's flower, Valour's tower, Fortune's Shame,
   England's Sun, Belgia's light, France's star, Spain's thunder
   Lisbon's lightning, Ireland's cloud, the whole world's
      wonder."

Here we have all the characteristics of Ophelia's lover : we have the courtier, the soldier and the scholar, the model for the whole world, and the flower of beauty as well.

There still remains for remark one portion of the death-scene of *Hamlet* ; that concerning the arrival of Fortinbras as heir to the kingdom, accompanied by his army. There is nothing whatever to explain this either in Saxo Grammaticus or in the *Hystorie of Hamblet* ; there could not be, as in both these accounts Hamlet himself takes the crown. Neither is there anything whatever in Shakespeare's *Hamlet* which explains why Fortinbras should be the heir. At the beginning of the play we are told by Horatio that Fortinbras lays claim to " certain lands " which his father had lost to the elder Hamlet, and was, therefore, threatening Denmark with war,[1] but Horatio never suggests that Fortinbras is, in any sense whatever, the heir of Denmark. Why should he be? He belongs to Norway, and not a hint is given us as to any legal or dynastic claim he may have on Denmark. Yet, in the last scene, Hamlet acknowledges him as his true successor.

Surely all this is very strange. The clue seems to me to be found once again in historical events.

It seems to have been an essential part of the Essex plot that James should be ready to support his claim to the succession by force of arms.

Mr John Bruce says [2] :

" It seems clear that Essex had been in correspondence with James ever since 1598. . . . Montjoy in the depth of his solicitude, . . . sent his Scottish Majesty a ' project,' the effect of which was that James should prepare an army, should march at the head of it to the borders and there fulminate a demand to the English government of an open declaration to the right of the succession, should support the demand by sending an ambassador into England, and of course, although not so stated, if his demand were refused, should cross the borders as an invader. . . . "

James was greatly grieved by the fate of Essex, and termed him his martyr. As early as November 1599, when under the influence of Essex, James procured to be suggested to his principal nobility of Scotland, that they should enter into a league or " Band " for the preservation of his person and the pursuit of his right to

[1] Act I., i.   [2] Introduction to *James's Letters*.

the crowns of England and Ireland. Such an engagement
was willingly entered into. . . .

He also solicited from his parliament . . . a liberal
grant for warlike purposes in reference to the succession.
" He was not certain," he told them, " how soon he
should have to use arms ; but whenever it should be, he
knew his right and would venture crown and all for
it. . . . The ' Band ' of the nobles was sufficiently well-
known in England."

I have already quoted Malone to the effect that the
last words of Horatio over Hamlet are the dying words
of Essex. Let us refer to the last words of Hamlet
himself :

> " I cannot live to hear the news from England ;
> But I do prophesy the election lights
> On Fortinbras : he has my dying voice ;
> So tell him, with the occurrents, more and less,
> Which have solicited. The rest is silence."

Surely it would be hardly possible to dramatise the
situation more closely ? We have the heir who belongs
to another kingdom altogether —a more northern one—
who is entering to make good his right at the head of his
army. We must remember that, when *Hamlet* was
written, it was still thought that such an armed in-
tervention might be necessary. Hamlet cannot live, as
Essex could not live, to " hear the news from England " ;
but he prophesies that the " election " will light on
Fortinbras and, in any case, he gives his " dying voice "
for him. Fortinbras commands that Hamlet's body
shall be placed " on a stage," a curious detail in itself,
and one that suggests the " stage " of execution.

Also, Fortinbras commands that full honours shall be paid to the body of Hamlet; and as a matter of fact, James did acknowledge his debt to Essex, for he restored his family to title and honours and set free his followers.

CHAPTER VIII

CONCLUSION

AND now, what is our main conclusion to be? It seems to me absolutely certain that the historical analogues exist; that they are important, numerous, detailed and undeniable. There are, however, three possible explanations as to how they get in the play:

(1) We may say that they belong to the "atmosphere" of the time and get in unconsciously. Shakespeare sees these things around him, and without knowing it, incorporates them in his drama.

(2) Shakespeare is writing a literary drama in which he incorporates a certain amount of contemporary history deliberately and of set purpose.

(3) Shakespeare is writing what is practically a piece of mythology; it consists mainly of contemporary history only fitted in to a dramatic frame.

Now, it appears to me that (1) may be rejected absolutely: the historical resemblances are so important on the one hand, so numerous, detailed and close on the other, that it does not seem to me they can have got in by any form of accident; when we reflect, moreover, that they were all events of *immediate* interest the supposition is practically impossible

To me the only choice lies between (2) and (3). I leave it to each reader to decide as to which alternative seems the more likely.

One thing seems, at any rate, absolutely certain, that Shakespeare is using a large element of contemporary history in *Hamlet*.

It appears to me that in the total construction of the play, the literary source is comparatively unimportant, and the historical source exceedingly important.

All the things that give us the essence of the Shakespearean drama are really historical; the secret murder, the use of poison, the voice of accusation heard in the night, the graphic representation reproducing the murder, the crucial character of Hamlet himself with his hesitancy and his reluctance to punish—the centre of the whole —the character of Claudius and his attitude towards Hamlet, the murder of Polonius, the character of Polonius, Hamlet's relation to the Players, the treatment of the Play which brings Hamlet's own neck into jeopardy, the love-story of Ophelia, the casket motive, the madness motive, the rivalry between Hamlet and Laertes, the way in which they are pitted against each other so that both may be destroyed, the grave-digger's scene, the fight in the grave, the entrance of Fortinbras—for all these no analogues can be found in the saga source (either Saxo or Belleforest), and very minute and close analogues can be found in the contemporary history of most *immediate* interest.

The Essex conspiracy and the Scottish succession were *the* questions of burning interest at the time, any audience would be certain to feel their appeal and

Shakespeare himself, as I have shown, had a double reason for a strong *personal* interest.

These events involved the fate of his dramatic company which was compromised by its connection with the Essex conspiracy and involved the fate of the man who was certainly his patron and possibly his dearest friend —Southampton—and who was even then in danger of death. Shakespeare desired to write about these subjects, and he *did* write about them, only he called them something else.

We have good reasons for believing that this method was fairly often followed.

(1) The authorities continually suspected the players of introducing political motives into their plays.

(2) Dr Haywarde was accused of having turned *Henry IV.* into a contemporary parallel.

(3) Shakespeare's company were accused of having done the same thing in *Richard II.* ; Shakespeare's own play.

(4) Shakespeare himself has shown us in Hamlet's treatment of the Gonzago play both how it could be done, and how dangerous it was to do it.

It seems to me that Shakespeare selected the *Amleth* saga in almost precisely the spirit in which Hamlet selected the Gonzago story. The *Amleth* story was sufficiently well-known to be excellent as a disguise, it was sufficiently remote to place no restrictions upon his handling, he was free to modify it as much as he chose, and he did modify it till there was hardly any of the original left.

It is not, I think, in the least difficult to see how

Shakespeare would naturally arrive at such a method of construction.

We cannot, I think, postulate with certainty many things concerning him, but there are two we do certainly know : one is that he was a man intensely interested in human nature as such, from the statecraft of kings and princes down to the ways of ostlers baiting their horses at an inn ; the second is that, as shown by such passages as the speech of Henry V. before Agincourt and the dying speech of John of Gaunt in *Richard II.*, Shakespeare must have been an intensely patriotic Englishman.

Such a man would naturally commence his career by attempting to dramatise history, a course which would gratify at once his love of reality and his patriotism. This is exactly what Shakespeare did in the long series of the historical dramas.

However, in the course of writing these dramas, he must have discovered that the choice of historical material unduly fettered his genius. Even in the historical dramas themselves Shakespeare is impelled to take great liberties both with chronology and with character.

Thus he alters considerably the age of Harry Percy to make him more clearly a rival to Prince Hal. In the second part of *Henry IV.*, also, the chronology is very curiously changed so as to convey the impression that the events occupy very much less space of time than they actually did occupy.[1] The space of eight years must elapse between the different portions of Act IV., but the impression given by the play is certainly that of a few days only.

[1] See my edition, *Henry IV.*, Part II. D.(C. Heath & Co., Boston, U.S.A.).

Nor is chronology the only difficulty. In history, the interest is too much diffused and is dissipated over too large a number of characters and incidents; it is distracted instead of being concentrated, and Shakespeare continually allows the dramatic stress to fall where the historic stress does not fall or would not naturally fall.

Moreover, it is possible that even here he allows himself to be deflected or, at least, influenced by contemporary events. Why, for example, is Falconbridge the real hero of *King John* ?

This is hardly true to the history of that reign even as the Elizabethans conceived it.

It has often been suggested that the prominence given to Falconbridge owes something to Shakespeare's sympathy for Sir John Perrot. Perrot, also, was the illegitimate son of a king, a soldier, a patriot, a man whose blunt speech got him into trouble.

In 1592 he was tried for high treason, and condemned to death, though his death in the Tower forestalled his execution.

This may, or may not, be the true motive for the prominence given to Falconbridge; but whatever the motive, there can be no doubt that Shakespeare lays the dramatic stress where the historic stress would not naturally fall.

In the two parts of *Henry IV.*, the same tendency is accentuated, for there is no doubt that the dramatic stress falls upon the character of Falstaff who certainly did not bear the historic stress; if we change the name to Oldcastle, the prominence given is less extraordinary, though still remarkable. Even here, it is probable that the desire to annoy Cobham, the Puritan persecutor of the stage and one of Essex's chief enemies, was a leading motive. At any rate, Cobham took it so ; he complained, the name was altered, and Shakespeare inserted an apology to the effect, "Oldcastle died a martyr, and this is not the man."

Both here and in the case of Falconbridge, it seems probable that we have contemporary events influencing even the case of the definitely historical dramas and producing a deflection of the historic stress. This was certainly the method the authorities suspected both in *Henry IV.* and in *Richard II.*

And now let us ask what a dramatist who arrived at this point in his artistic development would be likely to do ? He has an immense love for reality, he wishes to describe real life as it is actually lived ; his audience take an intense interest in the personalities and politics of the time, and having no newspapers, are particularly anxious to see them discussed upon the stage ; also the poet is patriotic, and wishes to deal with questions of national importance. On the other hand, he has discovered that history, as it is actually lived, is not really a good subject for dramatic treatment because its interest is too much diffused and its subject is too inelastic. Even if it were good material, which it is not, there remains the unvarying difficulty of the censorship which forbids him to make political references and has already, in *Henry IV.* and *Richard II.*, protested against his doing so.

The obvious expedient is surely to take historic material,

preferably those contemporary events in which he and his audience are most interested, and to alter them until they *become* good dramatic material, concentrating the interest, missing out all that cannot be got into a dramatic frame or which is irrelevant.

In this way a really excellent drama could be built up, only it would not be historic in the ordinary sense of the term ; the poet might, therefore, call it by another name ; in that case he would gain two great advantages.

(1) He would be able to modify the history as much as necessary to suit his artistic purpose. (2) He would be able to deal with contemporary events without falling under the ban of the censorship.

If this plan were followed, the first necessity would, of course, be to choose a novel or story whose outline resembled the one desired, and then to modify it freely just as Dr Haywarde was accused of doing in the case of *Henry IV.*, and just as Hamlet did in the Gonzago play.

As we have seen, it was a main count in the indictment against Essex that he had allowed and connived at this method of procedure, both in Haywarde's history and in Shakespeare's play of *Richard II.* Essex and Southampton, like Hamlet, both damaged themselves by their *political* association with players.

Shakespeare has the strongest *political* motive for treating history in this fashion ; he has also the strongest *artistic* motive, for a man naturally writes with more passion and fervour on subjects which interest him profoundly. Let us summarise briefly the way in which we have found political history to be used as material in the case of Hamlet.

(1) At the period when *Hamlet* was written, the two great subjects of universal interest were the question of the Scottish succession and the fate of the Essex conspirators; moreover, these two subjects were so intimately connected that they formed but one in the popular mind and, therefore, in treating them as one, Shakespeare would be simply working to a unity already existing in the minds of his audience. The fate of Essex and the fate of James have been blent in one destiny, and Shakspeare sees that, by blending them in one play, he can make a really magnificent drama.

(2) Shakespeare himself is particularly and passionately interested in both these subjects, not only as every patriotic Englishman must be interested in the fate of his country, but because the fate of his dramatic company has been involved in that of the Essex conspirators and because his best beloved friend is even then in danger of death.

(3) This theme, as it stands, cannot be treated under actual names, partly because it will only become dramatic *if concentrated*, and partly because the censorship will intervene if real names are employed.

(4) Shakespeare evades both difficulties by choosing as a disguise, the story of Hamlet; this enables him to concentrate the history and so turn it into magnificent dramatic material and it enables him, also, to evade the censorship.

(5) The process results in what might be termed a

" doubling of parts," so that one dramatic figure serves for two or more historic personages.

(6) Hamlet is mainly James I., but there are certainly large elements in his character and story taken from Essex, and probably some from Southampton. It is only the "melancholy" Essex of the last fatal years who could thus be combined with the more sombre James, and even so the character has been found by many eminent critics to be not psychologically consistent, and by almost all critics to be particularly difficult to interpret *as a unity*.

(7) Claudius, in the murder portion of the story, represents the elder Bothwell, in his relations to Hamlet the younger Bothwell; his attitude towards Laertes and Hamlet is that of Robert Cecil towards Raleigh and Essex. His character is largely that of the elder Bothwell as drawn by Buchanan, but with added elements of subtlety and treachery. Here again, the blending of the two subjects works into a unity.

(8) Polonius, in most of the relations of his life, is a minute and careful study of Burleigh, but his end is the dramatic end of Rizzio. Here again, the two subjects are blent into a unity.

(9) The play has two sources: the *Amleth* saga and contemporary history, of which the latter is by far the more important. The intense vibrating, passionate interest of the play is probably due to the fact that the subject was, of all possible subjects, the one most near to the poet and his audience, its eminently artistic form is due to the fact that the poet has moulded his material as much as he pleased, and that

his guiding principle has always been the artistic and dramatic effect.

If the account given above of *Hamlet* be really correct, then the play is mythology rather than psychology, or, perhaps, it would be fairer to define it as mythology on its way towards psychology. For a variety of reasons this seems to me inherently plausible. To interpret Shakespeare almost exactly as if he were nineteenth-century psychology is surely to thrust him out of his place in the order of development. The psychology of the sixteenth century cannot exactly resemble ours, and must have *some* points of difference. Why not this resemblance to mythology?

In the second place, as even such a thorough-going psychologist as Mr Bradley admits, some, at any rate, of Shakespeare's plays do produce very much the effect of ancient mythology. It seems to me that this effect is characteristic of a good many: that Shakespeare's Hamlet, his Lear, his Prospero, can hold their own even beside Achilles and Priam, Œdipus, Arthur, and Merlin. They are as universal and as romantic.

Now, we know that the great mythologic figures were, in all probability, created in some such way as the one suggested above. They were not copied by the poets from individuals, still less were they pure fiction; they probably represent accretions round some historic centre. Every student of early history knows the facility with which two or more historic figures become grouped in one, especially when they belong to the same family, or have the same name, or perform similar exploits.

Now, this mythologic method was quite well known

to Shakespeare's predecessors and contemporaries. As I have shown elsewhere,[1] Shakespeare's greatest contemporary—Spenser—writes what is practically a kind of mythology. He repeatedly[2] states that fairyland is really England, and that *The Faerie Queene* really stands for his own age and time. I think most readers will agree with me that *The Faerie Queene* looks even less like contemporary history than do Shakespeare's plays, yet we have the *repeated* assurance of its own author that it is.

Now, Spenser certainly seems to use the method I have described above : that of historic accretions grouped around some central figure. This is most obvious in Book V., where we are able to see with perfect plainness that Artegall must represent both Arthur, Lord Grey of Wilton, and also Leicester, for he performs both Grey's exploits in Ireland and Leicester's in the Low Countries. I have also endeavoured to show that the same principle applies with regard to the other characters ; that Duessa is both Mary Tudor and Mary, Queen of Scots, that Una represents sometimes the experiences of Anne Boleyn, sometimes those of Elizabeth.

Nor is the mythological method confined to Spenser ! A somewhat similar method is employed by Lyly, one of the dramatic predecessors who influenced Shakespeare most. Lyly writes plays which are ostensibly classical mythology, but which are in reality a kind of court allegory ; they represent contemporary characters, and contemporary politics in a classic disguise.

[1] *Faerie Queene*, Books I. and II. (Cambridge University Press).
[2] Book III.   Introduction, etc., see above.

Have we not been inclined to forget too readily how much of the mediæval mind still remains in the Elizabethans ? Why should not Shakespeare have a share of that which is so prominent both in Spenser and in Lyly ?

Yet, again, pointing in the direction I have indicated, is the example of Plutarch, who was almost a lay Bible to the Elizabethans.

He would direct Shakespeare's attention not to the study of *imaginary* characters, constructed on a psychological basis, but to the study of *real* characters of actual statesmen, with all their idiosyncrasies and peculiarities, and the mere idea of parallel lives grouped in pairs would suggest a grouping of such characters as the elder and the younger Bothwell, of Rizzio and Polonius, and also help towards the main conception—the parallel of Amleth and James I.

It would be, I think, unfair to say that Hamlet is the portrait of anyone ; he is more subtle, more interesting, more many-sided than any human being ever has been or could be. Shakespeare has taken from the story of James I. all that was most tragic and most pathetic, and from his character all that was most enigmatic, most attractive, and most interesting. He has taken from the story of James the Orestes-like central theme : the theme of the man whose father has been murdered, and whose mother has married the murderer. Shakespeare has also taken from James the central traits of Hamlet's character ; the hatred of bloodshed, the irresolution, the philosophic mind, the fear of action, the hesitation to punish which is half weakness and half generosity.

Only in Shakespeare the interest is concentrated as it is not in the history. In the history it was the elder Bothwell who murdered James's father and the younger Bothwell who held James in a kind of *duresse vile*, and threatened his life. By the simple expedient of combining in one the parts of the two Bothwells, Shakespeare gains dramatic unity and an enormous concentration of interest. The tragic motive of the father's murder is now brought into the closest possible relation with the tragic motive of the son's hesitancy and irresolution, and the two together make a drama of the most powerful and moving kind. What the story gains is what the stage so emphatically demands : compression and unity.

But this is not enough !

The tale of James I. is not finished and not complete ; nothing is rounded off. But the tragedy can be completed by uniting with it the tragedy of Essex, which, as we have said, is already one theme with it in the minds of the audience. By uniting the tragedy of Essex, Shakespeare gains a whole group more of most dramatic and interesting themes : the longing for seclusion and study, the desire to retire from Court, yet remaining obediently at the express wish and desire of the Queen, even the suit of "inky blackness" is reminiscent of the mourning of Essex as the populace had last seen him at his trial and execution. The feeling of profound melancholy, the longing for death, resembles that of Essex in his later years, so does the rivalry with Laertes, the sense of fatality and doom, it is in the terrible death which befell Essex that we have the clue to

M

Hamlet's shrinking from disfigurement and defilement after death.

It is from this source that we get the generosity and kindness of Hamlet's relation to the players, his tampering with the play and the ill influence this has on his own fate. It is because of this that we have the lack of ambition and the dying voice given to Fortinbras; these resemblances are pointed by giving us in the death-scene a quotation from the dying words of Essex. It is from this source, doubtless, that we have the element of the courtier and the soldier, the winning charm of personality which we are told have been prominent in Hamlet, for the last thing Fortinbras says of him is that he must have " the soldier's music and the rites of war."

If Hamlet were only the philosophic prince why this funeral, and why the body prominent on a stage to be seen of all the people ?

But the drama is still incomplete ! There is no love-story to add pathos. Now, here again, Shakespeare takes a motive which he may well have found in the drama of Essex, the motive of the innocent and loving woman cruelly used as a decoy, the motive of the stolen love-letters, stolen to injure the lover, but yet found to be love-letters, and nothing more, the motive of the bitter grief and wretchedness of the unhappy woman.

Possibly there is something added from the tale of Southampton which is so intimately bound up with that of Essex.

Ophelia sings a lament for " bonny sweet Robin," and this is the precise title Essex received from his mother and others.

The same method is employed with the other characters in the play. Burleigh was only recently dead. He had been the great opponent of Essex, he had plotted or was believed to have plotted against him, he had once refused the marriage of Essex and his daughter; Essex had certainly made Burleigh his butt often and repeatedly, and had taunted him recklessly and to the amusement of the whole Court; Burleigh, moreover, was supposed to have been the secret enemy of James, and was accused of tampering with the succession in favour of Spain. Burleigh, then, is the main original of Polonius, but he died peaceably in his bed, and such an ending is not really dramatic. Shakespeare gives us, therefore, the dramatic and dreadful death of Rizzio, and points the resemblance once again, as in the case of Essex, by an almost exact quotation.

Claudius is the two Bothwells; he is most closely drawn from the elder, and apparently, from Buchanan's picture of him, he has the drunkenness, lechery, adultery, incest, violence, meanness, cowardice, and personal hideousness which Buchanan declares to have characterised Bothwell.

Notwithstanding these facts, he exercised a curious and unaccountable fascination upon a queen who was already a wedded wife; neither Shakespeare nor Buchanan explain how, if he really was as they describe him, he contrived to fascinate the queen. Every word of Hamlet's terrific indictment of him is probably to be taken as true.

One may further ask: "Has Hamlet a political motive?" It is, of course, quite unnecessary to assume

M *

this ; the dramatic purpose, the mere desire to hold up, as Hamlet puts it, " the mirror to nature," " to show virtue her own feature, scorn her own image, and the very age and body of the time his form and pressure," this in itself is motive more than sufficient.

Nevertheless, it does seem possible that Hamlet may have, in addition to its purely artistic motive, a political motive also : that motive being simply the endeavour to excite as much sympathy as possible for the Essex conspirators, and for the Scottish succession, since it really was the accession of James which set Southampton free from the Tower, and restored Shakespeare's company once more to the favour of a monarch ; also it is more than probable that Shakespeare thought the Scottish succession would deliver the whole country from sub- servience to Spain.

In so far as Hamlet is James I., it seems to me that Shakespeare means to excite in us the desire to withdraw Hamlet from the Denmark which cannot appreciate him, and to give him a wider and a finer sphere. We know that James himself welcomed with all his heart his release from Scotland with its many restrictions, its many perils, and its necessity for endless subter- fuges, and welcomed the greater freedom of the English throne.

In so far as Hamlet is Essex, the political motive is to stress his own unwillingness for the life of courts and of ambition, his noble unsuspiciousness and the generous, but misplaced confidence which led him to his doom ; his instability of character is shown, his rashness, his passionateness, but through it all his nobility and the

pathos of his fate. Hamlet in death is singularly anxious
as Essex was anxious that his memory shall be cleared,
and the circumstances are admitted to be strange and
doubtful.

Now, if the method of construction be the one explained above, we can hardly expect to find a psychologic
unity in Hamlet, and I submit that, as a matter of fact,
we do not.

Take, for instance, Hudson's argument :

" In plain terms, Hamlet is mad, deranged, not indeed in
all his faculties nor perhaps in any of them continuously ;
that is, the derangement is partial and occasional ; paroxysms
of wildness and fury alternating with intervals of serenity
and composure.

" Now the reality of his madness is what the literary critics
have been strangely and unwisely reluctant to admit ; partly
because they thought it discreditable to the hero's intellect,
and partly because they did not understand the exceeding
versatility and multiformity of that disease.

" And one natural effect of the disease as we see it in him
is, that the several parts of his behaviour have no apparent
kindred or fellowship with each other ; it makes him full of
abrupt changes and contradictions ; his action when the
paroxysm is upon him being palpably inconsistent with his
action when properly himself. Hence, some have held him
to be many varieties of character in one, so that different
minds take very different impressions of him, and even the
same mind at different times. And as the critics have
supposed that amid all his changes there must be a constant
principle, and as they could not discover that principle, they
have therefore referred it to some unknown depth in his
being, whereas in madness the constant principle is either
wholly paralysed or else more or less subject to fits of paralysis ;
which latter is the case with Hamlet. Accordingly insane
people are commonly said to be not themselves but *beside
themselves.*"

A reference to a *Variorum Edition* will show that all the alienists take the same point of view, and consider Hamlet mad because he shows a " disharmonic psychology."

Now, it is exceedingly difficult to see how so many eminent critics could have taken such different views of Hamlet's character had it really been a psychological unity.

I do not think the case could be better summed up than in Hudson's words :—

"The several parts of his behaviour have no apparent kindred or fellowship with each other. . . . Hence some have held him to be many varieties of character in one."

Now, this is precisely the effect that would be produced in a mythological figure if Shakespeare were drawing from more than one character at the same time, and if these characters were such as not to amalgamate completely into a unity.   The same " disharmonic psychology," has been found by many critics in *Lear* and *Macbeth*, and by some in *Othello*.

The final conclusion I arrive at is that it is not advisable to think our study of Shakespeare's plays complete without careful reference to the history of his own time.

APPENDIX A

JAMES prided himself on being the destined restorer of the Arthurian empire. He offended both his Parliaments by styling himself, without the consent of either, King of Great Britain, and he desired, as Selden puts it, to get rid of the very names of strangers (*i.e.* Scotland and England). Masson says in his edition of the *Register of the Privy Council of Scotland*: "Nothing is more creditable to King James than the strength of his passion for such a union of the two kingdoms and peoples as might fitly follow the union of the two crowns. The intensity of his conception of the desirable union is not more remarkable than its thorough-going generality. . . .

"What had hitherto been the 'Borders' or 'Marches' between the two kingdoms were they not now simply the 'Middle Shires' of one and the same dominion, and ought they not to be re-christened by that name? Nay, why should the distinctive names of Scotland and England themselves be perpetuated more than reference to the past might make inevitable? Why should they not be known henceforth simply as North Britain and South Britain, integral parts of the same Great Britain? . . . By his own royal authority he attempted to abolish the names England and Scotland in all general documents."

James believed that the Gunpowder Plot was due largely to discontented subjects who disliked the union of the two kingdoms and the restoration of the Arthurian empire.

We may also compare the *Venetian State Papers* (April 17th, 1603):

" He will stay a few days in Berwick in order to arrange the form of the union of the two crowns. It is said that he is disposed to abandon the titles of England and Scotland and to call himself King of Great Britain, and like that famous and ancient King Arthur to embrace under one name the whole circuit of one thousand seven hundred miles, which includes the United Kingdom now possessed by his Majesty, in that one island."

APPENDIX B

The following is interesting as a commentary upon *The Merchant of Venice*.

It is an extract from the Burleigh papers, a portion of what appears to be an actual proclamation entitled: " An Account of Dr Lopez' Treason, 1593-4."

" Doctor Roger Lopez, a Portugall borne . . . he did use always the means of certain choice persons picked out by himself, in whom he reposed special trust, whereof a Portugall called Manuel Andrada was one, a man sometime attending on the King Don Antonio, both as their countrymen say, of one tribe and kindred. This Andrada, by letters intercepted, was discovered to have practised the death of the said Don Antonio."

[Andrada travels a great deal, to Spain and elsewhere.]

" He (Lopez) most wickedly did undertake a most

heinous purpose and resolution to take away the life of her most gracious Majesty by poison that had honoured him, a base fellow otherwise, with princely favour, rewards and good opinion.

". . . The precious life of our sovereign sacred Princess, upon whose life so many lives depend, should have been sold. Her life, I say, that giveth life to many, loath to take away the life of any, though by Law convicted; a sweet Lady, wonderfully inclining to Mercy, most loving to all Strangers; I may truly say, 'Decus et deliciæ mundi' the Jewel of the World. . . . This Stranger, made a denizen in the land, her sworn servant, would betray her beloved and dear life. . . . For the King of Spain, they say, so long as her Majesty liveth, distrusteth in the success of his intended purposes. . . .

"Now like wary Merchants (for their letters were written in style of Merchants), that these letters might be conveyed with more safety they communicated."

The document goes on to state how Elizabeth was referred to under the disguise of the Pearl: "Indeed this Pearl they mean though brought forth in a northern climate, yet far surmounting all the Oriental Pearles and Jewells, which the East or any other parts of the world ever had or hath."

Now here we surely have remarkable parallels to Shakespeare's play; there is first the disguise of the conspirators as merchants which suggests at once Shakespeare's title and general scheme. Then we have the praise of Elizabeth as the jewel of the world, far surpassing all others, as Bassanio praises Portia (I. i.), and we have the enthusiastic praise of her mercy ; we have the plot of the alien Jew ; we have the fact that the Jew employs to travel for him one of his own tribe exactly as Shylock employs Tubal.

Further close parallels—as, for example, that Don Antonio becomes a bankrupt, that he has to borrow money from the Jew Lopez even to pay for his clothes, that his vessels are lost, one by one or in groups, by fire, shipwreck, etc., in what seems an unprecedented run of ill-luck—can be found in the *State Papers*, 1593-4.

If the above proclamation were actually placarded on the walls of London (as it probably was) when Shakespeare's play was performed, the main significance of the drama would have been immediately apparent to all.

INDEX

187